LIFE *Amplified*

Lila Glasoe Francese

Wildhouse Publications

For Flissy & Matson
& Amara

Contents

* The use of "Volume" as a sub-chapter heading is both intentional and essential to *Life Amplified*. Each "Volume" progresses from 1 to 10 throughout the book, reflecting a gradual increase in resilience gained through the experience of loss. These headings punctuate the thematic arc of the narrative, illustrating that by moving through grief, one can ultimately live more fully, often at a higher volume than ever imagined or intended.

Prologue

"In the Lakota/Sioux tradition, a person who is grieving is considered most *wakan*, most holy.

There's a sense that when someone is struck by the sudden lightning of loss, he or she stands on the threshold of the spirit world. The prayers of those who grieve are considered especially strong, and it is proper to ask them for their help.

You might recall what it's like to be with someone who has grieved deeply. The person has no layer of protection, nothing left to defend. The mystery is looking out through that person's eyes. For the time being, he or she has accepted the reality of loss and has stopped clinging to the past or grasping at the future. In the groundless openness of sorrow, there is a wholeness of presence and a deep natural wisdom."

— Tara Brach

Chapter One — BELIEVE

Accepting the Death of a Loved One

"We can make ourselves miserable or we can make ourselves strong. The amount of effort is the same." — Pema Chödrön

2016

This is my first trip to Lake Tahoe without my sister Carolyn. It's our annual summer vacation spot. At Lake Tahoe, our family celebrates bad phone signals and a slow internet connection. It is our excuse to unplug. The magical lake is filled with cold crisp water reminiscent of the lakes I frequented as a child in northern Minnesota. Summer vacation revolves around this beautiful blue lake. We hunt for crawdads under the pier until we fill a whole bucket. Our kids open their eyes underwater and collect treasures from the pockets of the rippled sand floor. Sandcastles are formed using worn Tupperware that has occupied the kitchen of the lake house for decades. When my sister was dying from glioblastoma brain cancer, we brought her here twice. It was one of the few places she seemed peaceful. We shared deep thoughts on the shore, sitting in our Tommy Bahama beach chairs, hoping to tan our fair Scandinavian legs, sipping rosé, and digging our vacation-ready polished toes into the layers of cool sand.

This year, when we first arrived at the lake house, I could swear I saw Carolyn for a moment on the second-story deck smiling at our arrival. As of late, I've been seeing my dead sister's ghost everywhere, as if she were still alive. I smell her too. Her Jo Malone Orange Blossom perfume often lingers in the air as I enter a room. I heard recently that Albert

Einstein believed the layer between this life and the next is very thin. He believed this is why we still feel such a strong psycho-physical connection to those we have lost. It feels like my sister is not completely gone from my life, from our life, from our family. The kids randomly spot her too — at a swim meet or in a park as we drive past. My husband swears he saw her in the grocery store parking lot the other day.

It's 6:11 in the morning and the sun is just beginning to light the endless sky overhead. If I weren't on vacation, I'd already be swimming laps. This is my daily coping practice … each stroke of my swim working through my daily stress, my bad dreams, and my grief. This morning, I sit in the silence of the glass-framed living room that is as tall as the tips of the aspen trees. Lake Tahoe homes designed like this one are common. The bedrooms are on the lower floor and the living areas are on the second floor, so that guests can enjoy the picturesque tree-top views. I hear the faint crackle of the coffee maker as it warms up on the counter behind me. A slight chill in the air makes the expectation of a hot latte in my hand greater than most mornings. I walk lightly in stocking-covered feet because I don't want to wake my family. I love the feeling of being alone. Sipping from the clay mug I hold with both hands, I am aware of my heightened sensitivity to the newly awakened world. The leaves on the trees look greener than usual. The sunbeams hitting the wooden floor contain a whole spectrum of colors I don't remember noticing. The sight is dazzling and I crouch down on the floor to bask in the warmth of this spectacle. I breathe in deeply.

"I will not be afraid. I will not be afraid." I sing silently in my head. "I will look upward and travel onward and not be afraid." I learned this song thirty-five years ago at my childhood camp. The rest of the words escape me. These few lines have become my new mantra as I begin my morning meditation. My goal is resilience, finding some semblance of strength to get me through the day.

A month ago, while driving my mother to her income tax appointment, I was weighed down with an overwhelming reluctance to leave work. I feel resentful that I am solely responsible, now that my sister is gone, for being our mother's companion. I chauffeur her to her accountant's office, on the outskirts of our small town. At the first stop light, I look, out of habit, into the rearview mirror. My sister, Carolyn, is in full view in the car behind us. It is undeniable. Her blonde hair is styled in a long bob hairstyle, the way she styled it when she was a younger woman. Her face looks exactly the same. The car she drives is nondescript, almost like one of those random rental cars available only at the airport. I freeze. "Mom, pull down your visor mirror and tell me what you see behind us," I say with apprehension.

"What?" Mom answers.

"Just do it!" My urgent tone visibly rattles her and she pulls open her passenger-side visor mirror.

"Oh my goodness, oh my goodness," she repeats. "It's Carolyn." The light turns green.

"What do I do?" I bellow.

"Well, you have to drive me to the appointment, Lila."

"I know, Mom, I mean do I pull over now and see if she does?"

"There's the turn lane. Get in the turn lane, Lila." Mom motions to the left.

"Okay, okay but look out your window. She's going straight. See if she looks like her from the side too!" At this point, her car speeds past us on the right, and we are unable to see the driver. Mom and I pull into the parking lot. "Can you believe that?" I ask. I put the car in park. "I thought I was losing it. If you hadn't seen her too, I would think I was insane."

"I've heard of this kind of thing. But I never imagined it would happen to me," Mom says.

"I think she's telling me I'm not alone," I whimper, starting to cry. "Sometimes I'm so mad she's dead and I have to take care of everyone now. I swore out loud that she shouldn't have left me."

"Oh honey," Mom whispers patting my back. "She's still with us in our hearts, isn't she?"

"Yes," I answer. "And apparently in ugly rental cars too."

I thought we had all accepted my sister's death, but spotting her everywhere makes me wonder…

Acceptance, my first goal towards a resilient self.

Volume 1 — CHICKENS

"Realize deeply that the present moment is all you have. Make the NOW the primary focus of your life." — Eckhart Tolle, *The Power of Now: A Guide to Spiritual Enlightenment*

2008

My six-year-old daughter Fliss has asked for chickens. We recently moved to the small town of Ojai, California about an hour north of Los Angeles. After living in the big city for seventeen years, I'm tempted to fulfill her country-girl aspirations. I'm a Minnesota girl after all. My husband Dines grew up differently. He is from Santa Barbara and had a grandmother with a cook and a maid. He wouldn't like me to say it, but he looks privileged. I joke with him constantly that if his mother hadn't had a "plan for him," he would have been the perfect talk show host, reality show host, or maybe even an anchorman. He is tall, dark, and handsome. The best thing about Dines is that he is unaware of his appeal. Our big city life is now behind us and he feels totally at home in the country. Despite our disparate backgrounds, we come together as a well-tuned couple in these simple life moments. My desire for chickens emerged from fond memories of my Midwestern youth. Dines's desire to be a chicken owner is a bit of rebellion against his advantaged childhood. He enlists the help of a friendly neighbor, and the chickens we have been dreaming about soon arrive. They are a friendly lot, small enough for Fliss to pick up and pet in her lap. We all bond with them like we bonded with our Newfoundland, Colonel. Fliss has named them after her favorite cartoon characters from "The Backyardigans" (an adorable Nickelodeon animated children's show that centers on a group of five anthropomorphic best friends who use their imagination to embark on fantasies in their shared backyard). Fliss names her favorite chicken Tasha, after her favorite character on the show. We are told our new chickens are Araucana chickens. The eggs they lay are often blue. Checking the hen house each morning becomes a treasure hunt for our daughter, often resulting in three or four fresh eggs for our breakfast. "They are definitely earning their keep," Dines proclaims when Fliss shares her colorful eggs. We allow the chickens to roam often, and to the delight of Fliss, Tasha is a frequent back-door visitor.

"You can't bring her in, Flissy," I have to remind her. "But you can put her in your lap and sit at the outside table." Fliss follows my direction and she and Tasha spend countless hours together. Fliss pets her tufted feathers and Tasha leans in.

"Babe, Babe!" I hear, alongside an urgent arm grab one Monday morning.

"Huh? What are you doing up?" I answer. "It's barely light out." Dines sits on the side of the bed.

"They're all dead," he says placing his face into his hands. I spring up.

"Oh my God, who is?" I plead.

"The chickens," he says, shaking his head.

"Tasha?" I ask with trepidation.

"Yes," he moans. "Oh lord yes." All I can think of is Fliss and her immense love for this chicken. My mind races, searching for ideas of how to proceed.

"I'm calling her teacher," I proclaim, exiting the bed. Adrienne, the head of the Early Elementary Education Program at Fliss'ss school, is the fountainhead of knowledge about young children. Adrienne was the reason we moved to Ojai, so Fliss could attend the incredible Oak Grove School. The cars in the preschool parking lot have bumper stickers on them that say, "WHAT WOULD ADRIENNE DO?" Fliss is not yet awake and I quickly dial my phone. A half-hour later, Dines and I are en route to Adrienne's classroom, scones in hand from the local coffee shop as an alternative to our normal egg-collecting routine. Fliss leads us into the classroom. She is the first student to arrive. Adrienne motions for Fliss to sit on her lap.

"Good morning, good morning, good morning to you," Adrienne sings. "The day is beginning, there's so much to do. Good morning, good morning, good morning to you, Flissy."

"Good morning!" Fliss answers enthusiastically.

"Do you know why your Mommy and Daddy wanted you to be the first one at school today?" Adrienne asks.

Fliss shakes her head, "No."

"Well, your Mom and Dad discovered something surprising this morning and they asked if I could help explain it to you." Fliss nods. "Did you know we all have something in us called our soul, Fliss?"

"I have it?" Fliss innocently asks pointing to herself.

"Yes," smiles Adrienne. "You have it and I have it and Mommy and Daddy have it. We all have souls! Souls are what we are deep inside. It's our thoughts and our hearts and our feelings and all of our love."

"Wow," says Fliss. "That's all inside of me?"

"Yes," laughs Adrienne. "There is so much inside of you. There is way more inside of everyone than anyone can even see! We are what we are inside. Our bodies hold all these parts of who we are. But sometimes, after we have lived awhile, our parts don't need our bodies anymore. Our souls find a new place to be."

"A better place?" Fliss asks.

"Is that what you think?" Adrienne responds.

"Yes," says Fliss confidently, "definitely better!"

"It sounds like better is a great thing!" Adrienne exclaims. Fliss giggles. "Fliss, when your Daddy woke up today he found out that Tasha, your favorite chicken wasn't in her body anymore."

"She wasn't?" Fliss questions.

"That's right," Adrienne says. Fliss looks at me and I nod my head in agreement.

"She didn't need her body anymore," Fliss says, looking down at the ground.

"It seems that might be the case," Adrienne agrees. "And it's okay if we are going to miss seeing her in that body." Fliss starts to cry. "I see tears, Fliss. We see you are sad."

"I am sad," Fliss says coughing and attempting to talk through her grief. "I will miss her. I wish she said goodbye."

"I do too," Adrienne says stroking Fliss's hair. "I wish chickens could talk like you and me." Fliss leaves Adrienne's lap and crawls into mine. We hug for a long time and Daddy wraps his arms around us too.

"We will all miss our Tasha," I whisper in Flissy's ear, trying to hold back my tears, kissing her forehead.

A week later I pull into the early education parking lot and see through the fence that Fliss and four of her friends are standing over a dead hummingbird. "She didn't need her body anymore," Fliss says to the group.

"I wonder what she'll be next," says Rakesh, Fliss'ss Hindu classmate.

"She's just dead," answers Fliss's friend Chris, who comes from a secular family.

"Maybe she didn't do her mitzvahs," Fliss'ss Jewish friend Josh proclaims.

"I think I see her up in Heaven," Martie, Fliss's Christian friend says as she points upwards. "Right there, in the clouds!"

They are all digesting the death of the exquisite little bird in front of them. They are offering their ideas and beliefs about the situation. In their individual ways, at this moment, they have all accepted the bird's death.

Words Left Behind — Our Dear Tasha

Dear Tasha,

Though you were just a small chicken, your presence brought so much love and light into our little girl's world. You weren't just a pet—you were a friend, a source of laughter, and a warm companion to our child discovering the beauty of connection.

Your feathers, soft and bright white, and your gentle clucking offered comfort in quiet moments around our home. Through you, Fliss learned what it means to care deeply for another living being—to feel joy in nurturing and pride in watching you grow. Her favorite activity every morning was to check if you had laid eggs for our family. You never disappointed her and often produced double yolked eggs for our breakfasts.

Your time with Fliss was cut short, but even in your passing, you gave Fliss something invaluable—a first lesson in loss, and with it, the resilience of the heart. Your absence taught her about the fragility of life, but also how love for another living being doesn't have to end with a goodbye.

Thank you, Tasha, for being her first teacher in love and in life's bittersweet nature. You will always be remembered as more than a chicken—you were a cherished chapter in her story. You will be held dear in our hearts forever.

❧ Lila

Chapter Two — SELF CARE

Identifying Who/What is Taking Care of you both Physically and Spiritually

"Before Alice got to Wonderland she had to fall." — Anonymous

2008

The POD storage center is only thirty minutes from my house. It's a massive commercial building, bright orange in color, surrounded by an oversized parking lot. It has taken us almost a year since my sister died to retrieve her things. Carolyn was forty-six years old when she died. In 2014, at the age of forty-five, she was diagnosed with glioblastoma brain cancer. Despite receiving treatment and being admitted into a promising clinical trial, her life ended fourteen months after diagnosis. Her death drastically changed the path of my life and the lives of our family members.

At the POD storage center, we stop at the gate. I feel a familiar feeling of dread in my stomach, the memory of my sister's loss once again oozing into any available space in my body. My head begins to ache, and my palms are suddenly clammy.

"You ready for this?" Dines asks, raising his wide, dark Italian eyebrows upward while putting the car into park.

"Just give me a second, please," I say. Dines drops his hand from the gear shift and sighs. He grabs my hand and squeezes it. I use my other hand to stroke the soft hair on top of his forearm. "It still feels like she's on an art trip or a vacation."

"Yup," he agrees, and I look out the window. From the front gate, the view of the POD warehouse is even more daunting. It looks like a giant air conditioner, square and impersonal. The front door is flanked by a few indistinct plants, most likely a futile attempt by the management to make the entrance appear welcoming. It doesn't work. Nothing can warm up a giant metal building. Dines puts the car into gear and uses a code to open the gate. We pull into a spot in front of the entrance. I am still hesitant to open my car door, let alone actually enter the building. I keep my head down and say nothing. After sitting in my silence for a few moments, Dines says, "What if I head on into the office and ask that they bring the boxes out front?" I nod in agreement, "Okay."

I don't know how I would navigate this on my own. Dines is my superhero, stepping in to care for me in moments like these when I am unsure of how to move forward in the world. Most of the people who know us would be surprised about this. I have made a consistent effort in life to appear stalwart and unbreakable. Dines is one of the few loved ones in my life with whom I have relaxed enough to feel and be vulnerable. He disappears into the metal building for what feels like hours, but then re-emerges, his strong, tan arms holding an impossibly large box marked "CLOTHES" in my sister's cursive handwriting. Seeing it brings me back to a moment of innocence, two years earlier, when we rushed to pack up the last of her clothing. Her diagnosis came days later, at my house, where she was staying while remodeling her future home. These boxes have remained untouched since then. Seeing her handwriting, I realize she was the last one to touch the contents and tape the tops shut, and my eyes begin to fill with tears.

"Do you want to open them here?" Dines questions, opening the door and loading them into the back seat.

"Sure," I answer, wiping my eyes with trepidation. He uses the small red Swiss army knife on his key chain to gently slice into the tape atop the large box. As he tears back the tape ends and unfolds the flaps, the scent of my sister hits me. It is a mixture of her perfume, Jo Malone Orange Blossom, which still lingers on her packed clothes, and the scent of the leather from her belts and her shoes that line the bottom of the box. Carolyn excelled at packing—heavy items on the bottom of each box distribute the weight. I take a deep inhale that is audible to Dines. I can see on his face that he smells her too. Death affects all the senses. This is the first time my sense of smell has been allowed to grieve.

"I can't do this now," I whisper, the tears suddenly free-flowing down my cheeks. Dines closes the boxes.

"We'll put the boxes in the garage when we get home," he says. "There's no rush. You can go through them whenever you feel ready." I nod in agreement, not wanting to speak, knowing that if I do, the tears will escalate into audible sobbing. Dines loads two more boxes that the POD attendant has placed next to our vehicle. I buckle myself back into the front seat. He starts the car and reaches his hand to roll down the windows. I grab his arm.

"Leave them up, please," I say, choking back audible tears. I lean my head back on the headrest. I close my eyes, and for thirty minutes as I breathe slowly in and out, still ruminating on the smell of Carolyn's boxes. I am again with my sister.

It rarely rains in Southern California. This morning, a cloudy overcast sky sends a glimmer of light through my bedroom window. Dines tiptoed out of the house before sunrise to pick up our daughter from a school camping trip, and the empty house echoed as drops of rain hit the overhang on the front patio. When I am alone, it is hard not to think of my sister and feel her loss. I have slowly learned that staying busy is the best way to prevent myself from falling down the rabbit hole. Rather than staying in the warm embrace of my down comforter, I get up and pull on my favorite charcoal gray cotton drawstring pants and a black v-neck sweater, flung over the arm of the bedroom chair. I smooth clip my long blonde hair into a bun on top of my head and head to the kitchen for coffee. Food doesn't appeal to me in the mornings, but the first sip of my almond milk Nespresso latte tastes decadent. Holding the cup in both hands, I slide into my clogs by the kitchen door and head to the garage. Dines has placed my sister's boxes in a neat row against the side wall of the empty garage. We never park in this space, so the floor is as clean as the walls. My daughter's drum set sits in the middle of the space, ready for band practice on Wednesday night.

"Opening your boxes," I say out loud. I often talk to Carolyn when no one is around, still hoping she might answer back. I peel back a strip of clear packing tape and again, being hit by her scent, I fold down the flaps of the box. I begin removing items one by one, remembering, with each piece, a story. The green Versace silk dress was worn only once at last year's Art Basel in Miami. The black Louis Vuitton epi-leather handbag she bought after she sold a Diebenkorn painting to one of her art collectors. The pink Chanel cowboy boots she would never let me borrow. My sister had incredible taste. She was generous to others, but also to herself. It occurs to me that these pieces are now mine. I pick up her beige Everlane cashmere sweater and bring it to my face, rubbing it softly on my cheek and smelling it before placing it over my shoulder. I have never owned clothing of this caliber, except for a few items gifted to me on special occasions. I have never treated myself to such luxuries. Her belongings are comforting. Holding them is not painful. This surprises me. My anticipation of sorting through them was worse than the actual process. Carolyn was so good at taking care of herself. I feel like these boxes of her treasures are her final gift to me.

In America, I feel like we are easily obsessed with ownership of "things." This is ingrained in us early. At Christmas and on birthdays, we are told to make wish lists. In school, we buy things for "back to school time." We purchase items for our lockers, our dorm rooms, and our first apartments. When we get married, we gather a registry of all of the things we need to live happily ever after. Acquiring makes us feel good. We are taught that buying things is an acceptable reward for navigating this hectic world. Every young American girl is well-versed in "retail therapy." We watch movies about it. We read magazines and view social media accounts about the gratification shopping affords women. Buying, we are told, can help us counter the stressors of life. If I look good on the outside, no one will see what a mess I am internally. The more we are influenced, the more we want things, and it seems that all the pleasure we are promised will come from owning them.

This gift from my sister feels different. "You have no excuse now, Lila," I envision her saying. "Throw out your junk. You have all of my beautiful belongings." I take her imaginary advice, adding the pieces I remember fondly to my closet. It isn't the high style of Carolyn's clothing that comforts me. This is different than retail therapy. It's the fact that the clothing was hers and that every time I wear something of hers, I am again embraced by my sister whom I so deeply miss.

The following weeks pass in my now-familiar melancholy, punctuated by moments of profound sadness and flashes of joy-filled memories. Each day brings new thoughts of Carolyn, both sweet and painful. I find myself reaching for her clothes, her scent still on them, providing a healing balm for my heart. Dines, of course, is my rock through all of this, offering his quiet support without judgment. He understands my grief. It's complex. I am just beginning to fully express and process the loss of Carolyn.

On December 5th, 2017, I am awakened by the smell of smoke. I draw back the covers and quickly walk to the window. There is visible ash on the hoods of the cars in the driveway. I close the glass window panel that is allowing the smoky air to enter and return to bed to wake up Dines. "Honey, I think there's a fire," I say, shaking him slightly.

"Oh no," he answers groggily, turning over and looking towards the window. Dines and I have experienced fires before in Ojai. It is the reality of living in California.

"See if you can find anything on your phone," I say. "I'll take the dogs out." I put a sweatshirt over my tank top and leave the room to leash up the dogs. Outside, I am hit more forcefully than usual with the smell of fire. The sky looks dark, and I walk cautiously down the street, hoping to bump into another person who has more information than me. The street is empty, however, and as I venture further down the street, and closer to the creek near our home, I see billows of smoke. There are tall walls of bright red fire fiercer than I have ever seen. They scare me, and I quickly turn around and run back home. "Dines, Dines, wake up Fliss! We have to leave! I can see flames at the end of our street!"

"Are you serious?" he screams. I begin taking art off our walls, and gifts from my sister during her years as an art dealer and gallery owner.

"Grab my jewelry box! And the wedding albums!" I yell down the hallway at Dines. Fliss walks sleepily into the room holding her stuffed cat, Mimi. "Honey, get dressed!" I tell her, trying to remain calm. "We need to get in the car and get out of Ojai!" Dines barrels past me with piles of clothing, still on hangers, our wedding albums, my Burlwood jewelry box, and his collection of treasured skateboard decks.

"Let's get both cars loaded," he shouts, grabbing the leashed dogs and heading out to the driveway. For the next twenty minutes, every material object that is important to us is scooped up and transported to one of our vehicles. "The dogs are in the back seat of your car," Dines tells me. "Fliss and I will be right behind you. We have a reservation at a hotel in Santa Barbara." I walk to my car, putting the final items I have grabbed in my trunk. I realize I have taken a few precious things of mine, but almost everything that my sister left to me. I can't leave her behind.

We hit the road in a frantic caravan, our two cars meandering down Highway 150, guided by the faint glow of the menacing fire in our rearview mirrors. The air is thick with tension, and each passing mile brings a mounting sense of urgency. Fliss, clutching Mimi in the back seat, glances anxiously at the crimson sky.

In the hotel lobby of the El Encanto Hotel in Santa Barbara, an impromptu gathering unfolds among residents from our beloved Ojai Valley. They are also seeking refuge from the encroaching wildfire. The air is thick with a mix of worry and camaraderie as families, young and old, huddle together, faces reflecting both the weariness of escape and the shared resilience binding us all together. The room is alive with the soothing strains of acoustic guitars and the tranquil melodies of a grand piano, played by some of our fellow residents who have transformed this space into a sanctuary of music, laughter, and shared humanity. The notes weave through the air, allowing a brief respite from the collective anxiety that looms over us all.

As Ojai-ans, we sit and stand in small groups and share our harrowing escape stories. Extending my gaze over the room, the hotel lobby has become a makeshift living room for all of us Ojai folk, adorned with families and friends of all ages, suitcases and toys scattered about, and guitars propped against the walls. There is a sense of community happening in Santa Barbara that transcends our shared Ojai crisis. The dog tails are wagging, as they weave through the gathering, providing a comforting distraction from the uncertainty that awaits us all back home. Hands reach out to stroke a furry scruff or pat a welcoming canine head. A boy I recognize from Fliss'ss class sits at the piano, his quick hands massaging the keys as a young girl with a violin, nearby, begins to join in. A couple in their twenties strums their guitars in unison, their voices harmonizing with one another as others also join in, creating a communal sound that mirrors the emotions swirling throughout the room. Listening to the music, I am filled with sadness and hope, as I take in the familiar faces in the room.

For a brief moment, life continues only in this hotel lobby. The worries of the outside world begin to dissipate, and the exuding music becomes an anthem of sorts for our displaced souls. We bask under the warm glow of familiar camaraderie. Here, in the neighboring town of Santa Barbara, we find solace in each other's company, in the music, and in the safety of being together. In this random hotel lobby, we find strength in our shared story. Sleep comes quickly when we at last retire to our room and settle into our bed. It has been a long and grueling day. I am content to be safe, with my people, and alive.

In the morning, we are shocked to discover that Santa Barbara, our intended refuge, is also in danger of the ever-expanding wildfire. Overnight, the flames have engulfed the 150 Highway, and the air has filled with smoke. News alerts blare on the TV as we quickly re-pack and again on the car radios, detailing the rapid spread of the fire toward our supposed haven, the Belmond El Encanto Hotel. Panic creeps back into my body as reality sets in — we are being followed by a voracious inferno, the largest fire this region of California has seen in decades. Dines calls from his car to inform me that the road to safety is rapidly closing. We must move fast. I can see the flames under the overpass of Highway 101 as we drive out of Santa Barbara County, crossing the Ventura County border.

"Dines, what do we do?" I cry out over the car speaker, my hands gripping the steering wheel.

"Let's keep going. We can find another route and head towards Palm Springs," he responds. His voice is much calmer than mine. Palm Springs is the obvious choice. His family has lived there for decades. Fliss is seated in Dines's passenger seat, and I know she is safely buckled in with him until our next destination. We press on, the eerie glow of the flames casting long shadows on the hills next to the highway. Our now desperate need for safety motivates and propels us forward. The road trip is full of uncertainty and anxiety. I keep my eyes glued to the road as we head even further away from our home.

After a tense drive, we are relieved to solidify and find refuge in Palm Springs. It is a city far enough away to be out of danger of the relentless advance of the fire in our county. The familiar sight of palm trees, golf courses, and desert landscapes relieves us and replaces the images of charred hillsides back home. As we settle into our temporary sanctuary, a ranch we have visited for generations with family, the weight of our concerns hangs heavy for Ojai, but a newfound gratitude for the safety of our family creates calm.

For a week, Palm Springs shelters us in its arms. The desert provides a momentary and much-needed reprieve from the chaos we left behind. With each passing day, there is more news. The fire is named "The Thomas Fire." Its path of destruction is larger than any of us could have imagined. As the week passes, the incredible firefighters work their magic, the threat begins to diminish, and news of a possible containment provides us a glimmer of hope. Eventually, we are told we can return home. We wonder what we will return to in Ojai. I brace myself, not knowing what we will see returning to our precious valley. This fire has undoubtedly left an indelible mark on our family and the psyche of our community. It is a reminder of the power of nature and how vulnerable we are in its unpredictable path.

There is an incredible sense of community in Ojai when we return home. The business owners form a group and meet weekly to discuss one another's needs. Neighbors help neighbors, cleaning up the yards and homes on streets that were ravaged by the fire. We fled town worried about ourselves, but we have returned to Ojai concerned about our people. The Thomas Fire has opened a window of caring and generosity that we never expected. This catastrophe has revealed a light. Our town is amplified.

Volume 2 — *SUPPORT SOURCE*

"Find the helpers." — Mr. Rogers

2006

Mimi entered our lives in the winter of 2005. My daughter, seven months old at the time, often accompanied me on errands for my boss around Los Angeles. One of our favorite spots was Party On, a party store specializing in festive supplies and gifts. The store sold printed invitations, party goods, and assembled gift baskets with fillers like high-end candles and small, on-trend, home decor items. They also sold adorable stuffed animals by Jelly Cat, a brand I recognized from traveling in London. "Mimi," an elongated cat stuffy, was quickly swiped off a low-hanging shelf as my daughter's stroller passed the toy section. It was evident from the tight embrace of my tiny child that Mimi was now one of us. She had found a new home. The memory of "adopting" Mimi is so vivid. Fliss'ss eyes lit up with an unmistakable joy as she clutched the stuffed kitten, swiping her off the shelf. Her little hands grasped onto her soft, plush fur, making the store owner notice our eager purchase. He kindly offered a soft cotton cloth bag for Mimi to travel home in. It was the start of a beautiful friendship. As we left the store, Mimi tucked securely in her bag, I smiled, knowing that Mimi was more than an everyday, simple toy. This was "the toy" that would bring so much comfort and happiness to my daughter's life.

My preconceptions were true. By the fall of 2015, Mimi, the constant companion of my now eleven-year-old daughter, was barely a semblance of her former self. Her once fluffy beige and cream fur was worn and flat, exposing an odd bottom-heavy structure of the cat's stuffed center section. Her paws had flattened and the tail, also worn, was beginning to fray at the end. This was the result of deep love, co-sleeping, and frequent travel that involved being smashed into a suitcase, backpack, and occasionally the overhead plane compartment. Mimi had nursed colds and fevers, commiserated during time-outs, solved bad dreams, and served as a beacon of courage at sleepovers with Fliss's new friends. This year, Mimi wiped away tears of sorrow from the loss of my sister.

I have to admit, I am jealous that my daughter has her Mimi. How beautifully simple Mimi's purpose is in her world. When my daughter fell and skinned her knee, she cried out for what she needed—"Mimi." At bedtime, Mimi was tucked in too, a comforting companion as the lights were turned off and the house fell quiet. Children know how to ask for the self-care they need. Adults are more complicated. Our stuffed animals are eventually surrendered as we get older, and the security blankets that once trailed beyond us are put away. Many of us don't replace these comforting companions of our youth. More often, we replace them with adult comforts—shopping, eating, drinking, drugs, or meds.

After the loss of my sister, I am also guilty of this. My appetite is non-existent, and I am only able to manage three bites of food at most meals. But, I can drink wine every day, starting at four pm, sometimes sadly consuming a whole bottle by myself if no one is counting. Melatonin puts me to sleep because I am unable to drift off on my own. Advil medicates me again if I tragically wake up in the middle of the night. If I take pills, I don't think about my predicament. I don't process my loss.

There is no manual for grief. It wasn't until I was at the pharmacy looking for a stronger dose of Melatonin that I realized this cycle of self-medicating had to come to an end. I revert to what I have always done when paralyzed from moving forward. I read. I read every self-help book on grief I can find. I read and listen to experts online, from TED Talks to podcasts. I know that filling myself with knowledge about whatever I am experiencing will lead me through the pain. I learn the afterglow of a satisfyingly deep belly cry, like one of the books suggests. It feels good to get it out! Journaling is introduced to me, in an online blog, as a useful tool for grief. I write down story after story of experiences I shared with my sister. Reliving these moments in our history soothes me more than anything. My journaling has become a daily ritual, and my writing fills the void of a sleepless night like Advil and Melatonin did in the past. After one long late-night writing session on my living room sofa, I woke up embracing my notebook just like my daughter embraces her Mimi.

As I continued to voraciously journal, the process of writing began to transform my grief. I started to see my sister in the stories I penned, her laughter echoing in my memories, her presence becoming a comforting ghost on the pages of my notebook. Writing became a bridge to the past, a way to keep her alive in my heart. I wrote about the time we built a fort in the backyard, the walls made of old sheets and the roof held up by the branches of our favorite tree. I wrote about our late-night talks, whispering secrets under the covers, and the way she always knew how to make me laugh, even on my worst days and especially when I was scared of the dark. Carolyn was not scared of anything that I can remember, even when she was dying. She faced life and death head-on and with bravery.

In writing stories about my sister, I found solace. I found a way to accept and manage my grief. The act of writing allowed me to process my loss in a new, tangible way that I never expected. It was as if each word, each sentence, was a step forward, and a way to reclaim a part of myself that had been lost.

I can't read enough about loss. I find comfort in the wisdom of others who have walked this path before me. There isn't a lot available on the subject of glioblastoma, but I have discovered a few articles by grief counselors and psychologists, their insights offering a roadmap through the depths of sorrow. I listen to podcasts where people share their own stories of loss, their voices a reminder that I am not alone. These voices become a lifeline.

Amid my grief, I began to notice the small moments of beauty in my daily life. The way the sunlight filters through the trees through my window in the morning, casting a golden glow on the world. The sound of my nephew and my daughter's laughter, pure and unfiltered, is a reminder of the joy that can still exist after deep grief. These moments, fleeting and fragile, act as anchors, grounding me in the present and reminding me that life, despite its pain, is still full of charms and worth living.

As time passed, I began to integrate a writing practice into my life. I made a conscious effort to journal daily. I reduced my stress by taking time to nap, or at least rest my eyes in the afternoon. The children have started practicing mindfulness at their school. It's part of the progressive curriculum at their school. I am learning to be mindful too—present in the moment and appreciative of the here and now.

Transformation is gradual, but it can happen. We can slowly begin to feel lighter, as if a weight has been lifted from our shoulders. I can find joy in the little things, in the simple pleasures that I once took for granted. My sleep has improved. I can now naturally fall into a peaceful slumber.

Mimi has remained a steadfast companion for my daughter, her worn and frayed edges a testament to the love and comfort she provides. Seeing the bond my daughter shares with Mimi reminds me of the importance of having something or someone to hold onto, something to anchor us in times of turmoil. For my daughter, it is Mimi. For me, my mainstay is suddenly my writing. Transcribing my cherished memories, the love I have for my husband, my child, and the small moments of beauty that I have learned to take in daily are feeding my soul.

One night I write down a bold statement on the page in front of me: Grief is not something to be conquered or overcome. I am realizing that the journey of grief is a process that ebbs and flows like the tides. It is a part of life, a remembrance of the love we have for those we have lost. The pain of this loss may never fully disappear, but it will be transformed, and integrated into the fabric of our lives, making us stronger, more resilient, and more compassionate. When I think of Carolyn, I remember the moments of love so much more than the moments of loss.

In the quiet moments, when the house is still and the room is dark, I reflect on my journey through grief. The pain, the sorrow, the moments of despair are all a part of this story. But so are the moments of joy, laughter, and love. Life is beautiful, heartbreaking, and wonderfully human.

Words Left Behind — Thank you Mimi

Dear Mimi,

You've been with us for nearly two decades now, a soft and constant presence, and it's high time I thanked you properly. You may just be a stuffed animal to some, but in our family, you are so much more. You are a keeper of secrets, a soother of tears, a silent cheerleader, and an enduring reminder of love in its simplest, purest form.

I still remember the day we found you—or, rather, the day you found us at Party On. Flissy reached for you, on a lower shelf, in the gift section. From the moment her tiny hands held you close, I knew you were special. Her eyes lit up when she hugged you. Her joy spoke louder than the few words she could say, and from that day forward, you became part of our family.

Through scraped knees, sleepless nights, bad dreams, and big life changes, you have been her steadfast companion. You've traveled with us, been folded into backpacks and tucked into suitcases. You've borne witness to Flissy's happiest giggles and wiped away her saddest tears. When I couldn't always be there to comfort her, you were. Thank you for spending weeks with her at summer camp and four years in her dormitory at boarding school. For that, Mimi, I am endlessly grateful.

You've aged, of course. Your fur is worn out and no longer fluffy. Your tail is coming apart. But those marks of wear are proof of a life well-lived. They show how much you've been needed, cherished, and adored by our girl. You're a symbol of comfort and courage, a reminder that even in the hardest moments, there is something soft to hold onto.

Now that you've embarked on a new chapter, living away from our house, at Flissy's college apartment, I want to confess that I will miss you. You were always curled up on Flissy's bed and I am comforted knowing you're still by her side. The world is bigger and more complicated now, but some things never change. She says you are still sitting on her bed at her apartment. I am sure she still holds you tight when she needs to feel safe, just as she always has.

Thank you, Mimi, for everything you've done for her—and, in a way, for me and her dad too. Watching her hug you all these years has taught me the value of having a support source. In you, she found a lifelong friend. Love, no matter how worn and frayed, is always worth holding close.

With gratitude,

～Mamma Lila

Chapter Three — SHARE YOUR STORY

Escaping the Normal "I'm Fine" Salutation and Revealing Your Truth to Others

"Sharing your journey will lead you to the universal." — Brené Brown

2015

Throughout the fourteen months my sister was undergoing treatment for her brain cancer, I escaped for quick weekends to visit my best friend George in Salt Lake City. George grew up, like me, in Minnesota, and he was my roommate in our twenties in Los Angeles. It feels, in a way, like we grew into our adulthood together. I married him and his husband Brian. They are my daughter's godfathers. He has supported me through so many ups and downs in life like work, relationships, pregnancy, and marriage. He comforted me when my father died. George knows me better than almost anyone, and I love him like a big brother. A few weeks after Carolyn passed, I again fled to George's house on the outskirts of Salt Lake City.

George and his husband Brian relocated for George's job producing a news show for ABC. He goes to work early, and he often comes home very late. George and Brian have moved around a lot for George's job, but no matter where they live, their home is always a healing place for me. Brian, George's husband, is not only boyishly good-looking but an incredible cultivator of comfort living. He makes custom faux fur blankets, and when I arrive at their home, I am immediately swaddled in a new fluffy luxury product he has just hand-sewn. On every trip, we order Thai food, eat cinnamon gummy bears, and enjoy gourmet cheese. We have movie marathons. It's the perfect place to sleep-in, take a walk, or write in a journal. My daughter usually accompanies me to her Godfather's home, where our rules and routine from back home are often forgotten, and bowls of Froot Loops are consumed. This morning, she is still in a deep sleep in the lush "Brian-afied" bed I left a few hours earlier.

"What are you writing?" George asks as he enters the living room. The room is barely lit, and an outside light throws a faint reflection on the edge of the sofa where I am perched. I am typing feverishly on my small laptop.

"This is my journal, George. A grief journal, I guess, is what you could call it. It helps me get everything out. There's a lot I can't say in front of the kids."

"Does it help?" George asks, removing his glasses and cleaning them with the bottom of his blue cotton shirt.

"Actually, ja, it does." George puts on his glasses and sits down next to me on the sofa. We're both from Minnesota, and when we're together, our Midwest accents get worse.

"Can I read it?" George asks.

"You want to read my personal journal?" I gasp, pretending to be offended, closing it, and pulling it away.

"Oh please," he says. "You know you tell me everything anyway." He laughs. I nod.

"True," I agree. No one other than George could have asked to read my personal pages, but he's my closest friend, and I wonder if deep down he's trying to work out how to process the recent death of his mother, Orlu. He rarely talks about it, and if he does, he becomes emotional, pouring out deep feelings he has held back for a long time. I hand him my laptop. "It's all yours, Georgie. I'm going back to bed." I kiss his balding head and make my way to the guest room.

George is still reading the journal on my computer when I walk into the kitchen a few hours later. He doesn't look up while I pour a cup of coffee, so I pull a bar stool closely next to him and lean in over his shoulder. He looks up. I can see he's been crying. "This is good, Lila, but depressing as shit."

"It's my personal journal, George. Of course, it's depressing! The last year and a half hasn't been a walk in the park!" He closes the cover and begins tapping on the top.

"This could be an amazing book," he says emphatically. "You'd have to break up the sadness somehow… like with stories from your life before Carolyn got sick. Maybe childhood stories… something light and fun."

"So you're producing books now too, huh? Not just news and morning shows?" I laugh.

"I'm serious, Lila. You said you could barely find any articles on glioblastoma to read after Carolyn got diagnosed. This would be a story for people like you, in your position, I mean. People wanting to know what a journey through brain cancer would be like… what they could expect on their road through treatment."

"I've never written a book, George!" I exclaim. "I wouldn't know how to begin!"

"But you HAVE begun," George responds, holding up the laptop. "This is half the book! Share your story!"

I have experienced loss before, but I have never shared my story. I remember the first time I heard the word "cancer." I was seven, and I overheard my mother crying on the phone. Even at that age, I knew it was something terrible. The way she cried—a deep, hollow cry that seemed to come straight from her soul—told me that. Whatever this "cancer" was, it was bad enough to wound my mother just by saying its name. At seven, the concept of death never really crossed my mind, but I knew this cancer had something to do with it. "She won't be here much longer," I heard my mother say to my grandfather.

Grandma Vera was fading away, her small frame nearly disappearing into the bedsheets. I wondered if she might just vanish altogether, right before my eyes. And then, one morning, she was gone. I woke up, clutching my stuffed animal Pinky, and walked upstairs to her bedroom.

Grandma had evaporated overnight! So, this was death. Again, I heard my mother's deep, sorrowful cry. It was clear now—evaporating wasn't a good thing. I moved closer, and my mother pulled me into her warm arms. Her shirt was damp, probably from crying. In that moment, it dawned on me: if Grandma could die, maybe my mom could too. My tears mingled with hers on her flower-patterned turtleneck. We sat there, holding each other, for what felt like forever.

The aisle in the funeral home chapel felt impossibly long, the red carpet runner leading my sister and me toward Grandma's coffin. I was convinced she wouldn't be inside—she had evaporated, after all! But as we got closer, I saw her. She was dressed in a fancy yellow dress, with a matching hat, gloves on her hands, and flowers on her chest. "Touch her," my sister whispered, daring me. Hesitantly, I poked her forearm. Her flesh was hard, like a brick. She didn't feel like Grandma. So this is what happens when you die, I thought—they make a doll that looks like you. "That's not her," I said, looking up at my sister.

My mother came to gather us for the service. "Don't cry, Mama," I whispered. "She's not in there."

"Shhh," my mother replied, patting my knee. In my heart, I knew my grandmother wasn't in that metal box in front of us. But I sat quietly, letting my mom have her sad time with that doll that reminded her of her mother. From the lectern, the Lutheran pastor spoke about Grandma Vera's soul, explaining that it had left her body and it was now in a better place. I wondered if we'd ever visit this mysterious location to see Grandma again. I'd ask my mother when we got home.

Words Left Behind — My Grandma Vera

Dear Grandma Vera,

Even though you lived far away and I didn't see you as often as my other grandma, I miss you so much. I hope you can hear me, wherever you are now. Are you really gone? Mom says you are, but sometimes I wonder if maybe you just disappeared like magic or evaporated like when a puddle dries up. Do you live in a cloud now? Or maybe you're hiding in the stars?

Mom is really sad since you left, and I don't know how to make her smile again. Can you help her somehow, even from far away? I know you could always make her laugh, just like you made me laugh all the time. You were so funny, Grandma. Remember when you made me spit out my stuffing at Thanksgiving dinner because I was laughing so hard? I thought you were the funniest person in the whole world. Thank you for teaching me how to make homemade glue and spit watermelon seeds on the front porch.

I hope wherever you are, you're happy and maybe even laughing like you used to. It thundered down here last night and mom said that was probably you bowling with God. That sounds like fun. I'll keep trying to remember all the happy times you had here so Mom and I can smile more too.

Love you forever,

∽ Lila

When I was seven years old, I couldn't put into words the big emotions I was feeling. At eleven years old, when death visited my family again, I was able to talk about what I was experiencing. Losing Grandma Glasoe, my father's mom and my last grandmother alive, was the first death that made a massive impact on my life. She was an essential part of my everyday world. When I was very young, I spent afternoons at her house while my mother was working on her Ph.D. Grandma Glasoe loved what I loved—feminine colors like pink, dressing up in hats and pearls, and drinking cold root beer on a hot summer afternoon. I spent many days after school in her company, recounting my school day to her over

Skippy peanut butter sandwiches, served on the fine china she had spent a lifetime collecting. I remember feeling so grown up perched at the end of her grand dining room table where she always sat at holiday dinners. She taught me how to set a formal dining table (complete with butter knives and soup spoons), file my fingernails, and bask in the pleasure of an afternoon nap on the screened-in-porch. She called her soap opera, Days of Our Lives, "her story." If we had lunch plans after school, we always made sure to make it back to her house before "her story" started.

The phone rang early in the morning the day my Grandma Glasoe passed away. It was pre-dawn, and I could hear the scratchy sound of my father's baritone voice through my bedroom wall. Soon, the house lights were turned on, and the shadow of my father stood in my bedroom doorway. "Grandma's been rushed to the hospital." He spoke in a hushed, steady voice. "Get dressed. We need to get down there." I remember the panic of dressing fast, foregoing a new shirt, and instead just pulling a sweater over my pajama top. My mom, dad, Carolyn, and I clambered into our maroon Oldsmobile. My sister and I held hands in the backseat as my father sped down the streets of South Minneapolis.

Once at the hospital, we were escorted to Grandma Glasoe's room. She looked like she was sleeping and was hooked up to a machine that showed the beating of her heart. My dad spoke quietly to the doctor in the corner as I walked slowly to her bedside and touched her arm. It felt warm, but hard. I rubbed it back and forth, petting her while watching her chest fall up and down in synchronicity with the machine at her bedside. "I'm here, Grandma," I whispered closely in her ear. "We are all here with you." I could smell her Oil of Olay face lotion and I breathed in deeply, closing my eyes, softly kissing her cheek. She always let me have some of her face cream at bedtime when I had sleepovers at her house. Today, she looked as small as me lying on that hospital bed. I thought about yesterday, when we sat together, playing gin rummy and talking about the book "The Color Purple" that was soon being released as a movie. We spoke about how we would see it together, maybe even on opening night. Everything had felt so normal.

The doctor explained to my dad that my grandmother had had a heart attack at home, followed by a stroke in the hospital. This is why her right arm felt hard to the touch. If she woke up, paralysis would be evident on her right side. Her heart was pumping from a balloon the doctor had inserted in her chest as an assist. My dad was left with a heart-wrenching choice—additional surgery, which would entail major risks, or turning off her balloon pump, causing her, most likely, to pass away if her heart was unable to pump on its own. "Grandma would not want to live paralyzed," he told us. "I think we should say goodbye." I could feel the tears well up in my eyes. I laid my head next to Grandma Glasoe, again taking in her smell and how soft her cheek felt against mine.

"I can't say goodbye to you," I cried. "I need more time! I need you here with me." My dad rubbed my back, and I heard Carolyn leave the room, opening the door, most likely to join my mother in the hallway. "Can I have a minute, Daddy?" I asked.

"Yes," he answered, following the doctor out of the door. I didn't know what I wanted to say to her, but I knew these were my final moments by her side.

"I hope that being with Grandpa is where you are headed. I hope angels are true and they will bring you to him." Knowing how religious Gramma Glasoe was, I spoke the only religious words I could remember, "Matthew, Mark, Luke, and John, bless this bed that Grandma lays on. Four angels round her head, four corners of her bed, one to watch, one to pray, two to bear her soul away." It was the prayer she taught me when I had sleepovers at her house, and it seemed like it was full of the kind of church words she needed to hear at this desperate moment. I kissed her cheek again, and breathed her in one last time.

I don't remember Grandma Glasoe's funeral, or how many days I stayed home from school following her death. I do remember that when I returned to my classroom, I felt like the only kid who had ever lost a grandparent. "Did you see her actually die?" Taylor, my science partner, asked.

"Kind of," I hesitantly answered. "It was like she just quit breathing. Like she went to sleep."

"That's wild," Taylor said. "It's so weird how you can be here and then you suddenly aren't."

In the journal I keep as an adult, years after the experience of losing Grandma Glasoe, I write down all the details I can remember about her dying and the impact it made on me. I realize that I am cataloging my experiences of death. Recalling the losses I have lived through provides proof that I can survive the death of the person I am closest to in the world now, my sister.

When I found out I was pregnant with my daughter, I thought about the loss of my first grandmother, my mother's mom, Grandma Vera. I grappled with the concept of life and death, souls and bodies that no longer need us. I stared at the thin line on my positive pregnancy test, trying to imagine the new life, the baby forming inside me—appearing almost as magically as I believed my first grandmother had evaporated.

Words Left Behind — My Grandma Glasoe

Dear Grandma Glasoe,

I don't know if letters can reach Heaven, but I hope you're reading this somehow. Writing to you feels like the only way I can handle the huge, empty space you've left behind. You're gone, but I can still feel you everywhere. The hand lotion you always kept on your nightstand is now sitting on my nightstand, and the smell makes me think of you. I thought about you today in the afternoon when the light streamed through the kitchen window, how there was always a faint clinking sound of your bracelets when you did the dishes. I could swear I heard them today when I was loading the dishwasher. How is it that you're gone when you're still so much a part of everything?

Holding your hand in the hospital was the hardest thing I've ever done. It felt like my heart was being torn in two. Your hand was so still and hard, not like the warm, soft hand that always guided me through life. It's the hand that taught me how to shuffle cards for our gin rummy games, and the hand that would clasp your beautiful necklaces you let me try on. In those final moments, all I could do was hold your hand tight and tell you I loved you, even though you couldn't answer. I hope you heard my prayer.

You were my best friend, Grandma. It's not fair that you're gone! No one else in my class knows what this feels like. All their grandparents are still alive, showing up at holidays and school events. Why did you have to leave so soon? I feel cheated, like the universe is playing some cruel joke on me. I wasn't ready to say goodbye. I still need you! I thought we had more time—more afternoons sneaking root beer without Dad and Mom knowing, more shopping trips where you'd let me pick out something "fancy," more lunchtime talks where you'd share stories about how you grew up.

Your heart attack and stroke changed everything overnight. One day, you were glamorous and full of life, and the next, you couldn't speak. It was like watching someone dim the brightest light in the room. I know you are still teaching me things—about strength, about dignity, about loving fiercely even when everything is hard.

You were the first person to make me feel truly seen, understood and not like a little kid. You always knew the right thing to say, whether I was upset about a bad grade or nervous about performing at school. Who do I turn to now? Dad tries, but I know he's hurting too. Seeing him cry for the first time at your funeral broke something inside me. He never cries, Grandma. You were his anchor, just like you were mine.

I hope you're with Grandpa now. I hope you're laughing together and playing gin rummy in some beautiful place like the South of France. I don't remember him, but I am guessing Grandpa must have missed you so much. I know you missed him terribly. You're finally back with him! I hope you both can see me and that you're watching over all of us. I need you to be my angels, guiding me through this messiness of growing up. There's still so much I don't know, and I'm scared sometimes, but I'll try to be brave, Grandma, the way you always were.

I promise I'll keep you close. I'll remember everything you taught me—about manners, about cooking, and about finding beauty in the little things. I asked Dad to save your Wedgwood china for me. I promise to use it in my house someday to celebrate the big occasions. Thank you for collecting it for me. I won't forget you spent your dress allowance on it every month to complete the set. I'll always remember your hugs, and the way you tucked me in when we had sleepovers. I'll miss the gold fleur-de-lis wallpaper on your bedroom wall. When I miss you, I'll smell your lotion and think of you.
I love you forever, Grandma.

∽Lila

I lost my father in 2008. My daughter, Fliss, was four years old. My sister Carolyn's son, Matson, was almost two. My dad was an older dad, marrying my much younger mother when he was forty. I spent many years of my young life worrying that because of his age, he would die. He was the age of my friends' grandfathers. My father was a true Norwegian Viking. He was loud. He was a voracious meat eater, bragging that in his youth, he was often served four kinds of meat at dinner. He ate fat-filled Scandinavian specialties like Rullepølse and Blodpølse. My dad did not exercise in a traditional sense. He considered duck hunting, gardening, and ice fishing athletic. He was in bad health for the last decade of his life. His death, although a deep loss, was easier to navigate than either of my grandmothers. I had always anticipated that he would die, and when it finally happened, I was not at all surprised. My father was incredibly difficult to deal with in his final years. He was in pain from arthritis, burdened by his heavy weight, and I often worried caring for him would prematurely affect my mother's health.

Words Left Behind — My Viking Father

Dear Dad,

It has been sixteen years since you left us. Your presence is still felt. Your booming voice has worked its way into our everyday memories of you. I see hints of your Viking stubbornness in your grandchildren, Fliss and Matson. They regularly wave away my help and insist on doing things on their own. Fliss was only four when you passed, but she remembers you as a larger-than-life figure.

You were a true original, Dad, a Norwegian Viking to your core. Being a radio host was the perfect fit for your personality. They always played your robust version of "The Night Before Christmas" on KSTP at Christmas Time. You lived loudly and unapologetically. You were a true entertainer, with an appetite for life (and meat!) that was unmatched. You had scores of folks calling you for advice on how to buy and cook steaks. When I cook for Matson, I often think of your detailed stories about your mother's table, laden with four kinds of meat from your grandfather's butcher shop. You were always so proud of this fact. You'd "eat with gusto," ruminating on every bite. Your influence is apparent every time Matson cooks in our kitchen. He too is a food enthusiast.

You lived by your own code. You were difficult, of course, more so in the end. Your pain and frustration were not only heavy burdens for you, but for Mom as well. I worried endlessly about her, about how caring for you was wearing her down. You demanded a lot from her. I knew there was love beneath your exasperation, but I worried it wasn't enough. I think a part of her is still healing from her life with you. In my dreams, I have heard your apologies for your behavior and I have shared them with Mom.

When you finally passed, I wasn't shocked. I had been bracing myself for that day since I was old enough to understand how age worked. You were always older than my friends' dads, and that fact loomed large in my childhood, filling me with a constant fear of losing you. When it finally happened, I realized that all those years forecasting your death dulled the sharpness of your loss. It was easier, in some ways, to lose you, than Grandma Glasoe, though just as heartfelt. It was that I was older perhaps, more able in maturity to deal with the impact of death. I also, this time, was fortunate to have had my own family as support.

No matter how much I would like to deny it, you shaped me, Dad. Your creativity, your overt loudness, your quick wit, your intrinsic flaws are all a part of me. I miss you and carry you with me every day, in memory, in stories, and in the legacy you left behind.
I hope you have found peace.
All my love,

∼ Lila

After losing grandparents and a parent, the idea of facing another loss seemed inconceivable to me. When my sister received the devastating news that she had glioblastoma brain cancer, a terminal diagnosis, the reality of her diagnosis felt unimaginable. The thought of accepting what her tests and doctors said, knowing I would lose her in a few months— or if we were lucky, a year—cut me to my core. We were close in age. She did yoga daily and took walks; I didn't. She went on juice fasts after indulging in holiday food; I didn't. She never smoked; I did. The reality that my healthy sister was the one dying made the idea of losing her so surreal. I felt so far from death. I couldn't reconcile that she was walking into it. Our plans to navigate our adult life together, raise our children side by side, go on memorable trips with our families, and one day retire together were suddenly broken. Half of a lifetime would be all we had, at the end. I felt shattered.

Carolyn and I were always close. As young children, we were each other's first playmates and confidants. As the older sister, Carolyn was always my defender. Growing up, we had countless sleepovers in each other's rooms, whispered secrets under the covers, and concocted elaborate plans for our futures. We memorized all the words to every Barry Manilow album. We choreographed dances to the Bee Gees' hits. We held hands roller skating in our basement on cold winter days. Our sisterly bond strengthened as we got older. We fought as only sisters do, over stupid things like stealing one another's clothes, but we stood by each other throughout our teenage years, first loves, heartbreaks, the separation that happened when I moved out of state for college, and the trials that followed—getting jobs and beginning our early adulthood. When we both got married, our husbands, whose grandparents had known one another, became good friends, and our children, born soon after, became like siblings. Carolyn and I were more than sisters; we had grown into being one another's best friend.

In the aftermath of Carolyn's diagnosis, I had no appetite, a phenomenon entirely foreign to someone who inherited her appetite from her Viking father. The realization hit me—I had never been so profoundly affected by grief and loss. I had expected my father and my grandmother to die before me, and I had always imagined Carolyn and I would grow old together and eventually die around the same time. With the discovery of her brain cancer, my mind was filled with the scenarios of how life would change. My journal became a lifeline. I couldn't vent to Carolyn—God knows she had enough on her plate. But I could lay all of my frustrations, anger, and fears out on the page. Writing time became my sanctuary, a newly discovered form of self-help therapy through the written word. I didn't have solutions, but I found a way to create the story of our experience. The written journey evolved into a sacred catalog of moments, our story as sisters, my messy truth, and a front-line perspective that could potentially, as George suggested, resonate with others if I decided to share it.

The concept of turning my written confessions into a book had never crossed my mind before, but I found myself following George's advice and re-reading the pages and the daily entries. I realized it could become something worthy of publishing. It outlined an absolute, honest journey. It had become an introspective chronicling of my grief and had the potential to be a source of solace for those who found themselves in the same situation. Up to this point, writing was a hobby, not an activity that would elevate to book-length proportions. Writing suddenly assumed a new significance in my life. I found myself scheduling official time to write on my calendar. My writing time became more precious. When I was involved in a chapter, I found myself skipping events to stay home and write. For the first time, I contemplated the idea of being an author. It took the seismic impact of a devastating loss to uncover this piece of myself, to highlight a skill I had, that I had rarely called upon. "Can I call myself a writer?" I asked George over the phone one night. "I got the number of an editor and it felt so weird to leave a message on her voicemail introducing myself as such." George laughed. He was not only a great supporter, but a great facilitator. Not a surprise skill for a producer. He helped me when I was stuck laying out the book. His insights lit a light in me. I committed to a structure for the book and finishing a first draft, with his help and his constant reminder that beyond my story, the pages could be a potential source of connection and understanding for others grappling with loss. I joked with George that my mother would be proud that I was finally utilizing the skills of the rigorous academic prep school education she and my father had so generously afforded me. I decided to name my journal.

"Real books have titles, Lila," George remarked. I went around and around in my mind coming up with appropriate book titles. I even browsed titles of other authors' books online, hoping to find inspiration. Finally, I made a decision. The title of my book would be, "The Situation: A Radical Journey Thru Sisterhood." The name spoke to the life I lived with my sister and the profound thirteen months I experienced with her from her diagnosis to her death. It was a long and arduous year with Carolyn. We all were in battle together, fighting the worst diagnosis possible, glioblastoma brain cancer. As Carolyn's vocabulary dwindled, due to the relentless progression of her disease, she coined a term that became emblematic — everything was "The Situation." From mundane tasks like packing clothes in her suitcase, to navigating daily chores, she would simply say, "I need to deal with this situation." This phrase became the slogan of her journey.

Our sisterhood remains in my eyes the most radical and transformative relationship of my life. I am sure some of this was luck. Many siblings don't meld with one another as easily. Raised as the children of educators who worked long hours, we grew up depending on one another. Our lives remained intertwined as we left home, became married women and mothers. In forty-four years of sisterhood, we traversed more, experienced more, and built a connection that in the depths of unimaginable grief, grew stronger.

Carolyn chose to live in my home during her illness. She and Chris were remodeling their home, newly bought, across the road from ours, when she was diagnosed. She had been staying in our guest house above the garage while her house was taken down to the studs. Before her first surgery, her husband Chris asked her if there was anything she wanted when she woke up. She replied simply, "I just want my sister." So, post hospital and in between hospital treatments, Carolyn came home to me, and with her husband and her son. Carolyn used to joke that it was good she was the one who got terminally sick. "I don't know if I could have taken care of you like this, Lila. I probably would have put you in a facility." I would laugh, appreciating the fact her sense of humor continued during such a desperate time. Carolyn could have taken care of me. She was less patient than me, but she had a deep loving heart and knew how to manage anything.

"You would have done this so much better, Carolyn! The house would be in military shape if you were running the show."

Diving deeper into the pages of my journal, trying to formulate the flow of my book, memories flood back. I recall the many laughs, the tears we shed, the stupid disagreements as well as the countless times we leaned on each other for support. So many occasions stand out. We were stranded in New York City together on 9/11 after all of the bridges and tunnels were closed. It's the first time I realized that Manhattan is an actual island. Another example is when we got lost in Paris together trying to find a way back to our hotel. Carolyn learned she had lost a baby the day I gave birth to my daughter Fliss. That was a devastating revelation on one of the most important days of my life. Each journal entry I had written was a meaningful moment we shared in the trajectory of our lives. Some entries I re-read were more light-hearted than others, filled with laughable anecdotes of our sisterly antics. There were many deep, even somber, moments that added to the book too, reflecting the heavier experiences we navigated together. I still shudder when I think of how hard it was to deal with her when she was taking large doses of steroids. Steroids made her tumor growth slow down, but made her agitation grow to phenomenal proportion. Through it all, one thread stood out as constant in my writing: our underlying, unwavering love and commitment to each other, no matter the circumstance.

Piecing together chapters, I found myself staying up at night, so much later into the night than I ever had. The house, quiet, allowed words to almost spill out of me into the dark. "George," I exclaim one morning over the phone, "the process of turning my journal into a book is cathartic and so challenging. Sometimes, I write through my tears because the process forces me to confront my grief head-on. It's more difficult than I thought it would be to write about the painful moments."

"You need to remind yourself that the writing also allows you to celebrate Carolyn and the incredible woman she was," George says. "I never knew anyone with so much strength and resilience in the face of adversity. She excelled in her career as an art dealer, of course, but her perseverance through her cancer journey was beyond inspiring."

"George, do you ever think of the afterlife?" I ask. "I find myself thinking of it often, imagining, where the souls of family and friends I had lost now live. I wonder where Carolyn is living. I talk to my dead dad often, especially late at night, when I am writing. Are they together? Sometimes, I read my dad a section of the book aloud. Last night I told him that I hoped this book will honor Carolyn's memory. I confessed that I pray the book will provide Matson with a sense of who his mother was and how hard she fought to stay with him. I can almost feel my dad cheering me on, George."

"That's beautiful, Lila. He's helping you write your book. Carolyn is too," George proclaims.

"I guess that's the thing about writing—it allows you to hold on to what you've lost," I answer.

The cycle of writing and editing fuels me with a sense of purpose and determination. George's advice has sunk in. I know that this book is meant to happen. I am committed to seeing it through to publication. For Carolyn, for our family, and for everyone who has ever experienced the profound pain of losing a loved one, I vow to finish this book. It is a pivotal moment, to stand in the realization that I would never have written a book had Carolyn not gotten sick. The shock of her diagnosis and the harsh reality of her treatment and decline allowed me to look inside of myself for new navigational tools. I discovered a determined writer inside of me. To my surprise, my greatest loss has expanded my person. From my greatest loss, I am opening up and sharing this radical journey with the world.

Volume 3 — *ENDLESS STRUGGLE*

"Life IS an endless, truly endless struggle. There's no time when we're going to arrive at a plateau where the whole thing gets sorted. It's a struggle in the way every plant has to find its own way to stand up straight. A lot of the time it's a failure. And yet it's not a failure if some enlightenment comes from it." — Arthur Miller

I can't get the images of the day of Carolyn's death out of my head. I equate them with the reality that when someone famous who mattered to you dies, you know exactly where you were and whom you were with when you heard the news. My memories of that day repeat often in my dreams. The face of my mother entering Carolyn's room. The rare sound of my husband audibly crying. My biggest memory, however, is the image of my nine-year-old nephew Matson, walking into the room moments after his mother died. It was a monumental moment. I felt as if we were watching the innocence of his childhood disappear. To witness a young child grieve as deeply as the adults surrounding them is jarring. I remember feeling desperate—desperate to help, to comfort, to take away all the loss that was becoming Matson's reality. We were helpless under the powers of death, and the extent of grief never felt deeper. My nine-year-old nephew, physically collapsed as he audibly wailed over his mother's body. I was frozen. I felt desensitized, almost removed from the room, like I was watching a movie. I ached inside of places I didn't know I had inside of me.

My daughter, Fliss, two years older than Matson, bravely stepped in to comfort him. She embraced him, tightly, fiercely crying too. "I love you so much, Matson. I will always be here for you," she repeated time and time again.

When his wails subsided to crying, he forced out a response. "I love you too—so much Flissy—I will always be here for you too." None of the adults in the room intervened in their embrace. We stood still, in this abysmal moment, spent from the sadness but also taking in the beauty of their deep love. Matson and Fliss shared the kind of love for one another that day that could get them through anything.

No one can anticipate what they will feel or do in the moment they see someone they love die. We were not an exception. We had been anticipating Carolyn's death for over a year. But when, at last, the moment arrived, it hit our family with an unexpected force, harder than we could ever have imagined. There was no feeling of relief, only unimaginable loss and the reality she was gone from our lives forever.

It feels impossible to change the trajectory of life when the path was once so well planned. I am no longer a younger sister. I am the only sister. I have gone from "we" to "me." There is a new path in front of me. It isn't clear how I will proceed. I wonder if in the afterlife Carolyn will still feel like my big sister. I will live an earthly life much longer than she did, but is her soul continuing to grow where she is? I imagine titles don't matter after we die. Perhaps, the only importance will be our re-connection.

My sister's childhood friend Sanders asks to talk to Matson. He too lost his mother at a young age, and I know he is aware of the complicated emotions my nephew is going through. The emotion in Sanders's face, forty plus years after his loss, reiterates to me that grief is an endless struggle. It doesn't go away with time. Instead, life grows bigger around it.

Words Left Behind — My Big Sister, Carolyn

My Dearest Carolyn,

You are gone and I can hardly believe I'm writing this letter to you. It's impossible to put into words the enormity of what has happened, of what the world looks like without you in it. My heart feels broken. My body feels like I was hit by a barge. Part of me is gone, and I wonder if I'll ever feel whole again.

From the moment we heard the words "brain cancer," life as we knew it changed. Fourteen months is such a short time, but it feels like within that time we lived a lifetime of love and grief. In the absence of hope, with a terminal diagnosis, you faced every moment with grace and strength, and it was the honor of my life to walk with you through it. Caring for you, for Chris, and for Matson was the hardest thing I've ever done, but it was also the most sacred. I'll carry those moments with me forever. I am ruminating on the memories of sitting with you, watching the views from my windows or the waves at the lake. I am writing down our childhood memories and the outlandish stories you often embellished to the delight of our friends.

You were the best big sister anyone could ever ask for, always my protector, my confidante, my personal cheerleader. I forgive you for your temper—as I hope you forgive me for mine too—over the years. Working things out by shouting was the ugliest gift we were given from our childhood home. I always thought we'd grow old together, laugh about our wrinkles, reminisce about all the crazy adventures we had. It's impossible to imagine the rest of my life without you by my side. I can't fathom holidays without your stories or the smells of your delicious, masterful cooking filling the room.

I promise you this, Matson and Flissy will grow up together, as close as siblings. Our family will stay close, just like you would have wanted. Your wisdom will light our way. We'll keep telling stories about you— the kind and courageous woman who made art feel like magic, who made people feel seen and valued, who filled every space with culture and beauty. Matson will always know how much you loved him, and how fiercely proud you were of him.

We've decided to start an art foundation in your name. It's something I wish we could have done together, but I know you'll be with us every step of the way. Through your foundation, your legacy will live on, supporting artists the way you always did, championing their talents and creating connections that allow them to dream bigger.

Losing you feels like losing a part of myself. Maybe that's why losing a sibling is so devastating compared to losing a parent or a grandparent— because we imagine them with us for our entire lives. You've been with me for as long as I can remember. You know all of my secrets. Who am I without you? How do I go on without the person who knew me best, who shared my history, and my dreams for the future.

Thank you for introducing me to Dines. When you told me decades ago that you had "met my perfect husband," I was suspicious. You were right. He is one of the greatest gifts of my lifetime. I couldn't have dreamed up a more perfect partner or father for Fliss. I also want you to know these things: I will keep going full throttle, because I know you would. You'd want me to be strong for Matson and Fliss, for both of our families. You'd want me to try to find joy again, even if it feels impossible right now.

You are still there in the laughter of our children, and at the big events. We hung your stocking alongside ours this year. Losing you, just a few weeks prior, made it impossible to make any changes. I stared at the Christmas tree lights, long after everyone was in bed. In the quiet I could feel you with me and almost hear your voice.

Thank you for being my big sister. Thank you for the daily plethora of phone calls, the advice about running my own business, the fun we had time and time again, the love. Thank you for asking me to care for you in your final days, and for trusting me with the most precious parts of your life. I hope I made you proud. I hope I will continue to make you proud. You left me all of your beautiful things—your books, your jewelry, cherished art pieces, couture clothing—thinking they would bring me comfort. I treasure them, but the truth is, I have grown to realize "things" aren't as important as I grew up believing them to be. They're a poor substitute for you. Nothing material could ever fill the void you've left behind.

I miss you with every fiber of my being. I love you more than words can ever say. Until we meet again, Sissy, I'll keep carrying you with me, every step of the way.

Forever yours,

～Lila

My sister and I once took the kids to the opening of a new water park in San Diego. There was a ride that looked like a giant drain. Circular blue rafts rode on a water slide toward a drop that resembled the end of a faucet. Bravely, we buckled ourselves into orange life jackets and crawled into one of the rafts. We were instructed to hold a rope handle with both of our hands. As we approached the drain, I became filled with fear. The perspective inside of the ride gave us a much bigger picture than it had from the observation deck. How was it possible that this could end well? Wouldn't we flip the raft during our descent? Was our life in danger? "It's going to be fine," my sister bellowed over the sound of the raging water track. She had seen all of the color leave my face and my eyes widen. I held my breath. "You can trust the engineering," she yelled. She was correct. We fell from the faucet spout easily, slightly rotating as we moved through the air. We glided into a wide landing, circling the drain and the children giggled with abandon.

When finally, we settled at the bottom of the ride, I inhaled and exhaled and audibly screamed the words, "Thank you, God!"

The ride taught me an important lesson. A lot of life is out of our control. We have to trust the engineering instead of missing out on the experience.

The weeks following Carolyn's death found us on autopilot. The kids went back to school and reengaged in their friendships. Matson went to Joshua Tree on a school camping trip. We shared meals together, watched movies, swam in the pool, played with the dogs. We hosted a party in our backyard. There was food, wine, and live music. This party would also be the last big event we would host on the property. I sat, outvoted; the house was set to be sold.

"There are too many sad memories here," says Matson.

"We need a change," Dines chimes in.

"We don't need both of these big houses," Chris agrees. Eleven years has been the longest amount of time I have lived in a house in my adult life. There are so many memories I hold dear. The kids learned to swim in the pool. I held a summer camp for local girls in our meadow, when my daughter felt too shy to go to a day camp away from our home. There are still pieces of fairy furniture, made by the campers, in the trunks of our oak trees. I held countless dinner parties at our back patio table. Every Fourth of July, we hosted over a hundred people on our front lawn, viewing the local fireworks together. We had the perfect elevated front-row view. My daughter's band practiced weekly in our garage. My father slept in my guest room for a few months before he was hospitalized and passed away. We played charades with Carolyn, in this kitchen, every morning while she was sick, trying to figure out what she wanted to say, but couldn't articulate. I will be sad to leave this house. I wasn't enthusiastic about adding the stress of a move on top of everything else.

In my younger years, as my mother grappled with the decision to sell our childhood home, I failed to fully comprehend the depth of her sadness. To me, it was just bricks and mortar, rooms and hallways—a physical structure that housed us. What eluded me was the understanding that more than our bodies reside within the walls; our memories are intricately placed into every corner of our homes. Every mark on a door frame bore the imprint of a moment—my dad's wheelchair not making the turn into the guestroom, or one of our beloved dogs scratching to get out of the room. Pieces of the past surrounded us in every direction. The shoe I once threw at my sister in a fit of sibling frustration made a permanent mark on my childhood bedroom wall that was wallpapered in a white Laura Ashley flower pattern. I still remember the worn rug at the bottom of the stairs where our dog Kari found solace each night at bedtime—etchings of our shared history. Now, as I find myself in the poignant position of selling my home, I realize the weight of the memories. It's not just about parting with a physical space; it's bidding farewell to the repository of laughter, tears, and shared experiences contained within the walls. The home we sold held the markings of us all—my child, my nephew, my husband, our beloved pets, and the indelible presence of my sister. This home is part of our family, encasing the cherished memories that have come to define us. In home staging, which is part of my interior design business, we often say that furnishing an empty house makes it feel like a home. It's proved true. For the past eleven years we have been turning the empty house we bought into a home. I'm going to miss what we created, the changes we made to claim it as uniquely ours, the life we built in this place.

As the packing begins, I find myself more and more pensive about our future. How do we move forward, past the endless thirteen months we shared under our previous roof at the end of Carolyn's life? Our lives, once so neatly mapped out, are now full of uncertainty. Matson, still grappling with his grief, often seeks solace in the simple routines of his daily life. He is resilient, much more so than I was at his age. When we sit on the outdoor sofa at night, he asks about the stars, wondering if his mother is up there, perhaps sitting on one and watching over him. I tell him that in many ways, she is. The stars, like our memories, are reliable. They burn brightly over our heads every night.

My mom often says to me, "I know we are all feeling the deep grief from losing Carolyn. Life is full of struggles and some of them feel endless. But we will all survive this." It feels to me that I am doing more than learning to survive each day. I have come to realize that I am beginning to find meaning within the struggle itself. It sounds ridiculous but there is a peculiar beauty in the pain of loss. When I remember my sister I am not reflecting on her death. I am remembering the love, the deep, deep love that I felt for her, especially when she needed me the most and asked to be with me at the end of her life. Every day, I am reminded of her strength and her unwavering gusto for life. I know she would want me to "put on my big girl pants," (an expression she used quite often) and move forward.

"It's just stuff Lila," I imagine her saying. "Go ahead, pack it up." She would want me to "trust in the process," just as we trusted the engineering of that water ride. "There are new memories to make in your new home," she would say.

Carolyn believed her life had a pre-ordained plan. When it was your time to die, it just was. She spoke about it often after her diagnosis. "This isn't what I wanted for Matson," she would say. "But, it's just my time."

I remind myself that selling the house is not about leaving behind what was, but about making room for what will be. Letting go is not erasing our past, but rather, a tool for carrying us forward as we forge ahead into a new chapter. My struggle to let go is real. It is so intense. Every day I remind myself in my journal entry that the love, the memories, and the unbreakable bond that ties us together as a family will not remain inside these walls. We will take all of those important things with us to our new home.

Box after box, it is evident how much we have collected over the past decade. Each item I hold tells a story. The framed photographs, the children's artwork, the rows of books on the built-in shelving, my worn-out garden shoes by the back door—all fragments of eleven years well-lived and loved.

"Think of it as an edit," my mother says one day watching me pack spice containers in our kitchen. "You are always telling your design clients to edit and simplify. Now you are following your own advice."

"Ha, that's true," I concede, throwing some stale spice bottles into the recycle can. "Purging does feel good," I say. "Hopefully, this will feel like a fresh start."

There is change in the air, almost a restlessness in the rhythm of my life—the rhythm I have been moving to for the past decade. The children are forging ahead, and my life feels on the verge of slowing down. At least, I have the expectation that it will slow down.

My friend Peter, also known as "Vashaka," reads Vedic charts. He tells me I have been in the state of Rahu this past decade. Most people, he says, are a mess in Rahu. It's chaos. But for me, I thrive in a state of chaos. It's like being the one person who can get important things done while riding a roller coaster. But I feel as though soon, the roller coaster could stop. I am in the liminal state of now—between the chaos of the decade behind me and the quiet to come.

Every day, I attempt twenty-five minutes to rest my eyes. This has been crucial while in the process of packing. Sometimes I fall asleep, but usually, I am just still. I prop my feet up if I am sitting, or some days, I lie on my side on the sofa in my bedroom. I place a dark navy-blue silk tank top over my eyes. It is light in weight and makes the room turn dark. I sit in the sound of the room's stillness, my body's stillness, and I unplug for a small stretch of time. The house is often so quiet that I can hear the sound of my own swallow, the tone of my inner ear, and my pulse. I often count backward, steadying my breath until an easy rhythm sets in.

When I escape into a dream, I am delighted. The calm of watching the water on the shores of Lake Tahoe. Or the memory of the walks I took in our meadow after the rain, the leaves sticking to my rain boots and the fallen small twigs crunching beneath my step.

Twenty-five minutes of tranquility before the roller coaster heads for another loop. This has been my meditation, my respite. I always step back into action, recharged from the calm. The storm after the calm… Onward and upward.

I realize, compared to most, I'm doing life inside out—in my Rahu, in the chaos that is all mine.

Chapter Four — HELPING OTHERS

Developing an Awareness of Who is also Struggling

"The best way to not feel hopeless is to get up and do something."
— Barack Obama

2016

I met Lisa through my sister nearly a decade ago. She grew up in the Midwest, just like me, and later moved to Southern California to be closer to her family. Lisa's little girl, Amara, is just two years younger than my daughter, Fliss. As a single mom, Lisa faced the struggles that often come with raising a child alone, especially in the early years. It wasn't easy for her, but she managed with a quiet determination that I've always admired.

We share a similar aesthetic, and it felt like a natural transition when she joined the design business my husband and I started in our small town. Lisa quickly became indispensable—not just for her work ethic, but for her warmth and presence. Lisa's incredible smile, which lit up her whole face, and her soulful eyes that twinkled beneath thick, dark eyebrows captivated everyone. If Snow White were real, she would look like Lisa. Her personality mirrored the fairy tale princess too; she exuded kindness and compassion. I often joked that Lisa was my "hired patience" when dealing with difficult clients or uncooperative vendors.

Animals adored Lisa, just as much as every human who met her. My grandfather used to say you can tell when someone is an "old soul." That was Lisa—a wise old soul in the body of a forty-year-old mom.

There were days when I told Lisa to drop Amara off at our house so she could run errands "kid-free." Grocery shopping with a tired toddler can be a daunting task. Lisa always showed her gratitude by cooking us dinner when she returned, her meals a delicious blend of health-conscious ingredients and comforting flavors. Parenting young children is so much easier when you have a co-pilot, and Lisa was that for me. We had an unspoken agreement: we always have each other's backs. While she cooked in the kitchen, I sat and kept her company, as our little girls played dress-up and make-believe in the next room. Their high-pitched giggles echoed through the house, a sweet soundtrack to our friendship.

My relationship with Lisa evolved into a deeper friendship when she offered additional support to me as I coped with the death of my sister. She understood the deep-rooted bond between siblings, having two sisters of her own. During those months, Lisa cooked more dinners, moved her massage table into our living room to help treat Carolyn's pain, accompanied us on more outings, and offered more of herself than I could ever have asked for.

"We should volunteer at Sacred Beginnings," she suggested one afternoon at the design studio.

"What's that?" I asked, raising an eyebrow.

"It's a program at the Community Center that supports young families. They have this amazing infant care initiative where seasoned moms help new moms a couple of times a week."

I hesitated, unsure. "Lisa, I don't know if I'm in the right headspace for that. I'm still trying to manage things at home without Carolyn. Going from one kid to two is a big adjustment."

Lisa nodded empathetically. She knew how much I'd taken on, caring for my nephew and helping my brother-in-law. She stepped closer and placed a comforting hand on my shoulder.

"Sometimes helping other people is the best way to work through our own struggles," she said gently. "Let's just go to a meeting and see. Trust me—I think you'll like it." I don't know if it was her reassuring smile or the fact that I was too exhausted to disagree, but I found myself agreeing.

That Saturday, we sat on the floor of a classroom at Sacred Beginnings, surrounded by plush toys and toddler-sized furniture. Other women in the circle shared heartfelt stories about the young moms they'd supported. Their words resonated with something inside of me. For the first time in months, I wasn't consumed by my grief. I leaned over to Lisa during the lunch break and whispered, "You were right. This might be exactly what I need." Lisa just smiled, taking another bite of her sandwich, content to let me reach that conclusion on my own.

When my volunteer training was complete, I was paired with a family living in a yurt on an organic farm about thirty minutes away, outside of our town. Amy, the mom, was petite like me, with long, dark, curly hair and a familiar air of exhaustion. Baby Jacob, her three-month-old son, was big for his age, with chubby rolls on his legs that peeked out from his cotton onesie.

After washing my hands, I reached for the baby. Amy looked relieved as she handed him over. Jacob cooed softly, nuzzling into my neck. The feel of his warm, soft skin brought back vivid memories of holding my daughter as an infant. I whispered to Amy, "Why don't you lie down for a bit? You deserve a rest."

"Really?" she asked, her voice a mix of disbelief and gratitude. I rocked Jacob side to side, and softly nodded my head in agreement. She didn't need to be told twice, disappearing into the back corner of the yurt, where a plush king-sized mattress placed on the floor awaited her.

Jacob and I settled onto a pile of blankets a few feet from the entry. His tiny coos faded into soft breaths as he fell asleep. In the quiet, I began tidying up—folding soft fuzzy blankets, picking up baby toys and cloth books, and washing the mountain of dishes overtaking the sink basin. The act of cleaning, something I often saw as a chore in my own home, felt deeply satisfying here in the yurt.

Extending my time and energy to Amy and Jacob gave me a surprising sense of peace I hadn't known I needed. There was something healing about focusing on someone else, about being needed in a way that wasn't tied to my sister or the grief of slowly losing her. Lisa was right: sometimes, helping others truly is the best way to help yourself. I pulled my journal out of the tote bag I brought with me. The yurt sat in stillness as mother and baby slept, and I wrote eagerly about my gifts from the day:

"My hesitation to help blossomed into something beautiful today. It reminds me of the kindness and support I experience from family, friends, and even strangers stepping in with my sister. The strangers, especially, unburdened by the weight of a shared history, offer help that feels like the purest form of compassion … acts of kindness carried out for our family with no judgment or pity, only a genuine desire to lighten the load. Today I discovered a profound truth: healing isn't just about receiving help. It's also about finding strength in offering it to others. In the quiet moments of rocking a baby to sleep, washing dishes, or picking up toys, I am beginning to rebuild some parts of myself I thought were lost forever."

Volume 4 — WIDER FOCUS

"And those who were seen dancing, were thought to be crazy, by those who could not hear the music." — Friedrich Nietzsche

2016

I am not the first person who has embarked on a journey to find solace after experiencing deep grief. My sister, Carolyn, had been a prolific supporter of artists, a champion of creativity whose generosity shaped countless lives. She opened her first gallery in Minneapolis and, years later, another gallery in New York City. Carolyn specialized in cultivating private contemporary art collections, but the way she approached her work was unique in her field. Carolyn believed the artist always came first.

While many artists waited months for checks issued by their dealers after selling artworks, Carolyn issued payments immediately upon receipt. She cared deeply about the careers of "her artists," nurturing their growth beyond the scope of their contracts. She brought emerging artists to prestigious events, introduced them to collectors, and helped gather recognition for their names. At art fairs, she shared her hotel room with artists who couldn't afford the fees, ensuring they had access to the opportunities they deserved. Carolyn instructed artists to stay quiet about her patronage. She never boasted about her acts of kindness. While alive, her generosity remained unspoken and largely unacknowledged outside of her inner circle.

After Carolyn's diagnosis, as messages and emails began pouring in, I was overwhelmed by stories of her immense kindness. It turned out her generosity had been even more magnanimous than I'd ever been told or had imagined. She had gifted her old SUV to an artist so he could transport his work. She'd helped another secure gallery representation in his hometown, allowing him to move his studio out of his parents' garage. Carolyn bought a pair of couture shoes for an artist's wife, who, in her final months of pregnancy, felt unattractive and in Carolyn's mind deserved special acknowledgement. She funded art projects, sponsored museum openings, and became a coach, cheerleader, and therapist to those who crossed her professional path.

In Carolyn's final weeks, when it was clear her days were fleeting, I asked her if she had any regrets or unfulfilled dreams. I couldn't imagine she did. At forty-six, she had achieved more than most do in a lifetime. She had traveled widely, built a beautiful life with her husband and son, cultivated deep friendships, learned French, mastered culinary arts, made beautiful ceramics, practiced yoga and music, and left an indelible mark on the art world.

"I wish I had started a foundation," she told me one day, out of the blue, while we were sitting outside on my sectional sofa.

"For art?" I asked.

"For artists," she corrected me.

The distinction was significant. Carolyn's dream wasn't to glorify art as a concept but to uplift the individuals creating it. "I suppose you still could, Carolyn," I said softly, patting her back. "I don't know much about the art world, but we could find someone to help."

Her eyes brightened slightly, though the weight of her illness kept her words measured. The foundation wasn't a fleeting idea for Carolyn; it was her final ambition, the ultimate manifestation of her life's work. Within three months of her passing, my brother-in-law and I filed the paperwork to establish a nonprofit art foundation in her name. We had no idea how it would unfold, but we knew it felt right—a way to honor her and extend her legacy of generosity.

In the weeks that followed, as friends called to check on me, I shared updates about the foundation. These conversations often dissolved into bittersweet reminiscences—her hilariously exaggerated storytelling, her comical facial expressions, her warmth, and her fiercely generous soul.

One friend, who had recently moved to the West Coast, lamented, "I'm so sad she passed so soon after I moved here. She was the main reason I wanted to relocate."

"She was so excited you were moving closer," I reassured them. "She had so many plans for the fun times ahead with you."

Starting a foundation wasn't easy. My expectations of who would be involved and who would support us were quickly upended. Many of Carolyn's closest clients and friends were too overwhelmed with grief to engage with the foundation. One friend had a hard time even speaking with me on the phone. "I'm so sorry, but I need to hang up. You sound so much like Carolyn." To my surprise, our biggest initial supporter was someone who had never met Carolyn, but was inspired by our mission to prioritize artists. It was evident that this journey required building a new community, finding allies who shared Carolyn's vision. Along the way, I made new friends, for which I'm deeply grateful.

There is a secret cool factor about small town living that no one talks about. In Ojai, our little town of eight thousand people, our friends are all different ages, ranging from twenty-four to eighty-two. So while there may be fewer peers my age, there are opportunities to reach out to a wide array of people. Carolyn's foundation brought in supporters of all ages and backgrounds. The young kids, whose parents expressed interest in classes, had very little experience with fine art. One Cub Scout group I met with told me only one of the boys in the troop had ever been to an art museum. It was clear we needed to provide arts education opportunities in our youth community. I envisioned field trips to museums in close proximity. I dreamed of a space that would be large enough to hold classes with a great lineup of visiting artists I planned to invite. Our town also had a savvy art-loving community of retirees. They were hoping for more culturally enriching evening opportunities. My brother-in-law, Chris, and I knew we needed a space that could transform into a lecture hall or host a visiting art writer or even screen a film. We had a broad audience and big ideas.

On a bike ride home from the gym one morning, after swim practice, I noticed a FOR LEASE sign on a building I had ridden by many times. It was a fairly new condominium complex, and I never took much notice of it. On the ground floor of the front units, sat two commercial spaces. They were visible from the street. I pulled my bike up to the large picture window that held the lease sign. The space was empty, clean and had freshly painted white walls. It was more modern inside than I expected. I called Chris. "I think I found the perfect place for Carolyn's foundation!" I squealed over the phone.

We found out that the commercial, bottom floor space came with a two bedroom apartment above it. "This would be the perfect place for artists to stay," I remarked to Chris and Dines when we went to see it in person. Owning a design company would make furnishing the apartment easy. I had a consultation for a home staging job that afternoon, but made a mental note to run by our storage warehouse on my way home to see what specific items might work in the space.

I hadn't noticed earlier, but as I drove up to the address my navigation directed me to, I found myself outside the home my sister, Chris, and Matson once lived in before buying the property across our street. I took a deep breath, not knowing how I would feel going inside. Patsy, a lovely older woman, met me at the entry. "So nice to meet you," she said, extending her arm and shaking my hand. Patsy led me into the house and into the main living room. Before me sat many pieces of Carolyn's old furniture, pieces she had sold two years ago with the home. "We're moving to Telluride," Patsy said. "It's just too hot here for us in Ojai. I have no idea what to do with all of this furniture," she continued. "I've already shipped everything from our Los Angeles home to Telluride and we are sizing down tremendously!"

"Would you like help having a sale?" I offered.

"I'm not sure if we have enough for a sale, but I'd certainly be willing to just have someone pick what we aren't taking." The wheels began to spin in my head as my eyes darted around the room. The Italian chairs would be ideal for the foundation. The table with the surf resin finish would work perfectly for a desk.

In 2016, we officially opened the doors of The Carolyn Glasoe Bailey Foundation (CGBF), dedicated to supporting and advocating for the arts and sciences. The foundation space I had found was outfitted with many of the furnishing items Carolyn herself had purchased for her former home. Patsy had even generously donated some incredible art books. In the middle of downtown Ojai, our mission began. Our initiatives included awards for visual artists and The Ojai Institute, an artist residency program fostering dialogue between artists and the public through exhibitions, talks, podcasts, short films, and other programs.

One of our first projects was taking over a local student art show from a gallery in town that could no longer host it. The process was simple yet meaningful: local students submitted artwork through their teachers, and the teachers forwarded the selections to us for consideration. Our foundation then curated the final participants and work. It was a way to engage young artists and honor Carolyn's belief in nurturing creativity at all stages.

"Mom, what can I do at the foundation?" Fliss asked one afternoon. "I've been to so many museums and galleries. I bet I know more about art than most kids."

Her words rang true. Fliss and her cousin Matson had spent countless hours accompanying Carolyn and me on art trips. Once, during a tour of a New York collector's apartment, the kids identified many artists' works before we even received the handout listing them.

"How would you like to be the Student Art Show Curator, Fliss?" I suggested. Her eyes lit up, and she smiled sheepishly.

"You'd help pick the artwork for the show and assist the students with their bios," I explained. Over the next few days, Fliss threw herself into the task, designing a poster, contacting participants, and diagramming a layout for the exhibition. Her enthusiasm was infectious, and I realized the foundation had become a vessel for passing Carolyn's legacy to the next generation.

As the waves of my grief came and left, I found comfort in my work at the foundation. I felt connected, still, to my sister. The foundation not only amplified Carolyn's impact, but also enriched the lives of those closest to me. Fliss began curating her own art collection on her bedroom walls. She volunteered at our events, checking people in, helping to serve food, or selling raffle tickets. Matson shared the foundation's mission with his Boy Scout troop, emphasizing what he had learned— that becoming an artist is as noble an aspiration as pursuing medicine, law, or teaching.

Through the foundation, I inadvertently became an architect of new possibilities, drawing Carolyn's passion for art into the core of our lives. In honoring her legacy, we discovered a powerful truth: even amidst profound loss, there exists the potential for big transformation, compassionate connection, newfound creativity and a future illuminated by those we lost. The trauma of losing Carolyn and then the pivot to create something meaningful has led to this moment. Focusing on what we can do breathes new life into our bodies.

Chapter Five — HUMOR

Finding Joy in our Lowest Moments

"You may encounter many defeats, but you must not be defeated. In fact, it may be necessary to encounter the defeats, so you can know who you are, what you can rise from, how you can still come out of it." — Maya Angelou

2008

My friend invited me to attend a local fundraiser for an African nonprofit organization. As part of my recovery from Carolyn's passing, I've been making a conscious effort to keep myself occupied, or more honestly, as busy as possible, especially in the evenings. There are very few people I know at the event I am attending. Apparently, the organization's Board of Directors has traveled into our little town to attend, and there is only a small sprinkling of Ojai locals. The night starts with beautifully catered appetizers and fine wine, passed around by a uniformed catering staff. The home, owned by a board member I know minimally from social events in town, is one of the larger homes in town. It is decorated with obvious souvenirs from his many trips around the world—African textiles, robust colored platters, bespoke instruments. The walls of our gathering space are thick stucco, and the sound of guests chatting and laughing bounces off them, creating an echo effect in the room. I sip cold German white wine and pop squares of smoked Gouda cheese into my mouth.

The music is turned down, and there is feedback from a microphone being handed to a distinguished gray-haired gentleman on the steps leading into the room. "Please find a seat," he says into the microphone.

Scanning the space around me, I identify a built-in bench and sink into its canvas-covered seat cushion.

"Is this seat taken?" says a slender, older, attractive blonde woman standing in front of me.

"No," I smile. "Please, go ahead." I motion to the space beside me.

"I'm Linda," she says, flashing a warm smile and extending her hand.

"Lila," I say. "Nice to meet you."

"Have you been to Africa?" Linda asks.

"No, unfortunately not," I say. "My friend is the new Development Director, so I'm just here to support." I take another sip of wine.

"That's what you think," she winks. "I think our meeting is meant to be!" Linda clinks her glass to mine and also takes a sip.

Over the course of the scheduled program, I see incredible scenic pictures of Africa—Kenya, specifically. I hear stories about lions, leopards, and wildebeests, incredible animals I can only imagine seeing in person. I discover that Linda, my bench mate, is a trustee of this organization and she travels annually to Kenya.

"It's my second home," she offers. "I have found a sense of peace in Kenya that I haven't found anywhere else." Linda's uncle, she tells me, was one of the original big game hunters in Kenya. "You have to meet him!" she exclaims. "He's fascinating. He's in his nineties now and has decided to donate his land to this nonprofit when he passes. He's turned into a passionate protector of Kenya's wildlife in his later years. We can stay on his land. His son has built a beautiful lodge. Give me your email and I'll send you details."

I can't explain how I convinced myself or my family to let me take a three-week trip to Kenya, but somehow I did. I agree with what Linda told me when we met: I think we were supposed to meet. Her invitation opened up a new world for me, a place I had never in my wildest imagination dreamed of exploring. After my sister's death, Africa became an otherworldly refuge of space and healing, a reminder that I am just one small, five-foot-three speck in this massive world.

"The scale of Africa is outrageous," my friend Sanders tells me in the school parking lot while we wait to pick up our kids. "The elephants and giraffes don't look as large in Kenya as they do at the zoo. They are enormous, but they fit in with the massive scale of everything." My excitement builds. I realize I haven't looked forward to something so much in a very long time. Linda tells me I can invite a friend, and my friend Tonya agrees to accompany me. We buy plane tickets, schedule the required vaccinations, and pack carry-on bags in anticipation of the trip.

The weeks pass quickly in anticipation of my trip. The morning I leave, my house is quiet. The sun has not yet risen, and the sky is filled with a plethora of stars lighting my way to the car that is picking me up. Tonya is waiting outside as we approach her house. "Let the adventure begin!" she laughs to the driver, hoisting her suitcase into the trunk. Tonya is the perfect companion for this journey. She is a seasoned traveler and tells me, immediately after I extend the invitation, that she has always dreamed of going to Africa. She's as busy as I am. Tonya is a well-known broker and real estate agent in our town. Our hours of travel include work for both of us. Tonya knew my sister, but she doesn't dwell on the topic (like so many do) when we're together. She's confident, grounded, and just the kind of company I need. I am committed to working on my writing while we travel, and Tonya is so swamped with real estate contracts that we find ourselves perfectly in rhythm with one another.

The next night, we arrive at Nairobi airport. A representative from the nonprofit organization meets us and helps quickly process our entry papers and passports. The airport is open-air and filled with crowds of people. A scarf over my head covers my blonde hair. Although her hair is darker than mine, Tonya also wears a scarf. This was a suggestion in our trip paperwork. Apparently, exposing our lighter hair could hold us up at the airport. "People will want to touch your hair or have a picture taken with you," we were told. I am relieved to have a guide assist us through the airport and quickly into a van.

Our first stop is in the suburbs outside Nairobi, called Karen. This charming area is the setting for the book Out of Africa, written by Isak Dinesen (a pseudonym for Baroness Karen Blixen) about her time in Kenya from 1914 to 1931. Her coffee plantation, the Karen Blixen House, is now a hotel and our home for our first night on the continent. The furnishings are as romantic as one would imagine from seeing the movie based on the book. There is mosquito cloth cascading over the top of my four-poster bed. Beautiful vases in my room spill over with roses. Tonya tells me her room is just as charming. The grounds are lush and vibrant green, and a gentle breeze billows. The wind hits the metal roof of the building, creating a melodic sound that sends a faint whisper throughout my room. I linger in the warm shower after our long flight and fall asleep quickly, bathed in new sounds.

The following morning, I wake up early to the sun peeping through my vintage, wood-framed window. Breakfast includes eggs with bright orange yolks, almost fluorescent in color. I have never seen eggs this bright. The coffee is incredible. We learn our hotel has a history as a former coffee farm. Tonya and I meet up with the rest of Linda's group before we depart for our next destination. Tonya, an easy conversationalist, soon has us feeling like we are among friends. We're all from diverse places in the United States and hold a variety of interests: an entrepreneur, an artist, a filmmaker, a real estate professional, a writer/ designer, a physical therapist, a retired professor, a poet, a lawyer, a non-profit professional, and a philanthropist. Once again, we are loaded into a van, on our way to the local airport.

Our highway journeys expose a lot of Kenya to me that is new. Kibera is just outside of Nairobi and we are told it is one of the world's largest slums. The shantytown appears to be built on miles of garbage. Linda says she believes it houses almost one million people. I have never seen poverty of this scope. It appears endless. I find myself thinking back about the conversation I had with my friend Sanders about the size and scale of everything in Kenya. Kibera is massive and we are all silent, staring at it, taking it in mile after mile, while we pass at high speeds.

At the airport, we are greeted by Daniel, our pilot, who will fly our private charter plane to Lewa, the home of Linda's nonprofit organization, in the heart of northern Kenya. I've never been on a small plane, and my heart begins to race immediately. There are four rows of cloth-covered red seats and a seat up front solely for the pilot. My palms begin to sweat as we buckle in and prepare to take off. I am seated directly behind the pilot, offering a full view out the front window and the left side as well. Linda, perhaps seeing my apprehension, whispers over my seat, into my ear, "Being a pilot is one of the most revered jobs in this part of Africa. Young men study long and hard for this position. We are in good hands."

The sky is blue and tranquil, dotted with picturesque clouds. Luckily, I am still tired from traveling, and closing my eyes in anticipation of takeoff results in an impromptu nap.

I wake to see land directly below us. The plane lands smoothly on a dirt runway, kicking up dust as the wheels touch the ground. We will be staying at Lewa Safari Camp. Vans meet us to transport us and our luggage. When we step into the van, Linda gives us a brief introduction.

"Welcome to Lewa! My second home! We are so lucky to have arrived by plane. The roads here are often not paved and very treacherous. We would never have made it by ground. This 140,000-acre reserve is committed to preserving the land and ecosystem of the area. Take it in, it's absolutely my favorite spot on the planet."

We are told there is poaching surveillance and elephant-proof fencing on the property. Our greeter is Francis, a very tall Maasai guide who will introduce us to Lewa. He is dressed in traditional clothing adorned with nine handwoven colorful bracelets and an intricate headpiece. Maasai men traditionally wear bold jewelry, and it's as striking as the landscape itself.

An ostrich greets us at the entry of the camp, and ten minutes into our ride in the Land Cruiser, we encounter another greeter—a young male lion resting under a shade tree. Apparently, when we ride in the Land Cruisers, the animals see us as one large moving entity rather than individual humans. We are told we are safe in these cars, but to of course keep our arms inside the vehicle. The accommodations are stunning. Thatched roofs blend seamlessly with the natural scenery, and small, colorful birds chirp happily in the trees. The African Superb Starling is particularly striking, with feathers painted in iridescent blues and oranges. Nature's harmony in Kenya brings me a sense of contentment, as though I have temporarily fled from my colossal grief to a place where I feel small and humbled in comparison to the vast scenery.

As the sun begins its descent in Kenya, the temperature shifts dramatically, and a sudden coolness washes over the wild land. Wrapped in soft wool blankets draped over our shoulders, we savor cocktails affectionately called "sundowners," by the locals. My body feels warm after swallowing a few sips of the concoction. It is the perfect accompaniment to the crisp evening air. Looking out over Lewa's rolling hills and how they stretch out before us, I notice they are dotted with promontories perfect for gazing at the extraordinary view. The sky here feels endless. It is breathtaking, reminding me of the images of heaven I have dreamed about since Carolyn died. Within its boundless expanse, I feel an unexpected closeness to my sister's spirit. Perhaps Heaven is closer to Kenya than it is back home. The dusk sets in sky before us, so endless and eternal. I am comforted in its presence, held in its embrace.

The landscape teems with life in this part of the world. The majestic acacia trees that have stood watch for centuries, frame the plains where exotic animals roam in packs. It's easy to imagine ancient humans standing where we are now, marveling at the ancestors of these creatures before retiring in the same ridges and valleys standing before me. I imagine the land itself whispers stories of its past, and all those who came before. Kenya exists beyond the bounds of ordinary time, a place where life flows in an unbroken, cyclical rhythm, echoing an eternal promise of renewal and continuity.

Tonya, my steadfast companion, shares funny stories over sundowners, her voice hitting the high and low notes of each tale, creating a joyful connection with our group. In private, in our shared thatched roof cottage known as a "nyumba," she is careful not to ask too much about my year of loss, a silence for which I am deeply grateful. Here, amidst strangers and within the serenity of Lewa, I am not yet ready to share my recent history. Instead, I am committed to absorbing the healing energy around me, allowing Kenya's timeless beauty to work its quiet magic.

Animals seem to appear at every turn on this trip. Each moment holds a new revelation. The Grévy's zebra, unfamiliar to me until now, captivates us all with its unique patterns, each one a masterpiece of individuality. Unlike the classic black-and-white Burchell's Zebra, the Grévy's are striped in shades of brown and cream, their bat-shaped ears and large heads lending them a whimsical, stuffed-animal quality. I can't help but think of my twelve-year-old daughter, who would be utterly enchanted by these creatures, begging to take one home.

The Burchell's Zebras, with their more familiar stripes, move together in tight-knit herds. Our guide tells us this is a coordinated dance of survival. He explains that the animals, moving en masse, as we drive in our Land Rover, appear as a single, massive entity. This keeps them safe from unwanted charges by other creatures. I wonder if this instinctual understanding of strength in unity is a natural reaction or if the zebras are taught the concept when they are young. Instinctively or not, they know that together, they are stronger, safer—a poignant metaphor for our own lives.

It is September, and the ponds scattered across the landscape are shallow, not yet deep enough for the hippopotamuses. The zebras gather in their great herds along the pond shores, drinking from the life-giving water. Our guide tells us that the short rains will arrive in November, transforming these shallow pools into deeper, more vibrant oases. The anticipation of this seasonal shift underscores the cyclical rhythm of life here, a reminder that everything, even the arid stretches, will eventually give way to renewal.

From the back seat of the bumpy moving Land Rover, I am struck by the unrelenting vitality of the life around me. Lewa Safari Camp, our refuge in this vast expanse, feels like an extension of the landscape itself. Its thatched roofs blend seamlessly with the natural surroundings. The color of the nyumbas matches the color of the landscape. There is a palette of browns, tans, and golds reaching far into the horizon. The air is filled with the sounds of melodic chirping. A small colorful bird is perched near our entry and is impressively loud for its tiny size. Every element of nature seems meant to be. The small bird is loud because he has a lot of territory to reach with his calling. Unsurprisingly, we learn that everything here is interconnected, from the ancient trees to the symbiotic relationships between the smallest creatures.

One of the most exhilarating moments of the trip comes as we witness the great wildebeest migration on the border of Tanzania. Linda tells our group that she has been hoping to see it live since her first trip during migration time in 1978. We are fortunate to be staying among a wildlife documentary team from the BBC. They have confessed to us that the wildebeest expert among them thinks the migration is imminent. We park on the shore of the Mara River alongside the BBC vehicles. We wait three long hours, hoping that the wildebeests lingering in the distance will suddenly mobilize and brave the river crossing into Tanzania.

"What do you think, Lila?" Linda bellows from the front row of the Land Rover.

"About what specifically?" I answer.

"Do we wait it out longer? I'm leaving it up to you!" she says emphatically.

"We've been here for a good amount of time already," I answer. "It seems to me there's no harm in waiting another half hour until we need to head back for lunch."

"Good plan!" Linda exclaims, extending her right arm up into air as a punctuation. Not even two minutes later, the sound of the wildebeest herd rumbles the ground below us. The mass of the herd is unbelievable, the end nowhere to be found. The sight of the migration is breathtaking—a raw and primal display of survival as the herds navigate the treacherous river crossings, teeming with crocodiles and hippos. It is both brutal and awe-inspiring, a testament to the resilience and determination of the animal life in Africa.

In the heart of Kenya, surrounded by creatures both great and small and beneath the endless expanse of the African sky, I feel a re-awakening. This trip, the longest of my life, began with an unexpected encounter at a fundraiser. Linda's invitation—a quiet yet insistent call—opened a door to this healing pilgrimage. Linda offered me this sanctuary and I took it.

As our Land Rover rolls across the bumpy landscape, headed back to camp for lunch, I close my eyes, listening to the rustling of the tall grass beneath us, the distant calls of the African birds, and the exuberant conversations within our group about what we have witnessed. I will always remember this time in Kenya, with its ancient history and extraordinary beauty, and how it became a healing balm for my sad soul. In this moment, in the shadows of the African plains, I realize this truth: joy can bloom in the most unexpected places. Even in the wake of our deepest losses, it can rise, unexpectedly in unknown waters, filling our innermost selves with light and hope.

Volume 5 — CHARADES

2015

As my sister navigated the final stretch of her terminal journey, her once-vibrant vocabulary had dwindled to a handful of simple phrases and words. The gravity of her brain cancer transformed our household into a makeshift care-center, where we faced serious struggles with a touch of humor—a coping mechanism that became shared language. Carolyn's words may have grown sparse, but in their brevity, they carried a gravity that stretched beyond mere conversation.

Our family had become a living support system, our home a cocoon of sorts that enveloped all of us—Dines, Fliss, Carolyn, Chris, Matson, and me. Chris, occasionally on the road for work, and my husband commuting daily to an office nearby, made my self-employed design job the most flexible to meet my sister's needs during this challenging time. Despite the gravity of the situation, Carolyn and I found solace in the absurdity of moments throughout each day. It was as if humor became the glue that held us together, allowing us to laugh even as we grappled with her terminal diagnosis. Life had simplified inside the walls of our home, turning into a celebration of small accomplishments. I wore my emotions on my sleeve. I felt raw. Carolyn was becoming more fragile day by day. I bravely said things I thought I would never need to say.

"Thank you, Carolyn, for helping me. For my whole life, you have been a second mother." Small tasks we had taken for granted we now accomplished together. I ran her baths because she had trouble turning on the faucet. I applied make-up for her because her vision was disappearing in one eye. In the midst of her struggle, there was beauty in our intimacy. There were final memories made with one another that I would hold onto long after her death.

Amidst her linguistic struggles, Carolyn's creativity, surprisingly, flourished. Forgetting names became her whimsical game, where I was sometimes referred to simply as "sister." Chris, her husband, often momentarily lost in the web of her damaged memory, became known to us all as "the other sister."

"Why am I the other sister, and you're not the other husband?" Chris would protest.

"I've been here longer," I'd reply. Given the absurdity of our situation, we would often erupt in laughter, echoing our shared plotline. When friends witnessed the "unique title" Carolyn had afforded Chris, their expressions of shock amused us. Our humor, now unorthodox, had become a lifeline for our family. Even Carolyn found joy in the irony of her linguistic gymnastics, always quick to join us in deep belly laughs and share in the experience.

"Ridiculous!" she would often exclaim, a burst of glee escaping her lips as she tried to comment on her struggle to find the right words. It became her common refrain, a rallying cry against the hurdles that her damaged brain enacted, challenging her to communicate. To address her challenge of communicating, good old-fashioned games of charades slowly emerged in our home. Figuring out Carolyn's needs with her hand signals and colorful nonsensical vocabulary, oddly became a source of delight. We played charades with unabashed enthusiasm. The hours we spent engaged with Carolyn, trying to figure things out, became a poignant dance of connection.

Carolyn, in her frailty, got a kick out of our deciphering games. There was a flicker of amusement in her eyes when she came up with a word before we figured it out through her hand signals. The family member who solved the puzzle of what Carolyn was trying to communicate was met with cheers of Olympic proportion. Our creative sleuthing brought lightness to the underlying heaviness that hung in the air. I learned that laughter is desperately needed in the tough moments of life. It is vital relief in a weighted moment, offering sustenance to weary souls. Charades, in its simplicity, became our powerful love language. It felt so good to connect. Amplifying the funny moments with one another saved our spirits in those final weeks of Carolyn's life.

Carolyn's illness stripped away so much—her independence, her words, the life she and Chris had built—but it also revealed the bare essence of who she was: someone who could find humor even in the face of despair. My mom commented that Carolyn's laughter was such a relief to hear when she was so sick. The funny moments of shared joy felt like found treasure. Life's beauty isn't diminished by its brevity. We only had forty-six years with Carolyn, but our memories are filled with so many moments of laughter and love.

I remember, quite often, Carolyn's vibrant spirit. She would point to herself and say, "Still here," her eyes twinkling with mischief. It was her way of reminding us—and herself—that she was more than her symptoms and her diagnosis. That even as her words, eyesight, and body began to fail her, her essence remained intact. And in those moments, it felt like she was teaching us something profound: that life, even in its most fragile state, is still worth celebrating.

The final days—a blur of desperate struggle, quiet goodbyes, and intimate moments—was underscored by the laughter that lingered. When Carolyn passed, the house felt unbearably silent. I missed hearing her laugh. It took a very long time as a family to recount Carolyn's most absurd and hilarious moments. For years, the weight of losing her weighed us down. I couldn't speak about her without becoming emotional. I cried hard and often. I needed to. It was cathartic.

I often find myself wondering why, when we all know intrinsically that we are dying, the death of one person impacts us so profoundly— often more than the loss of another. When my Great Aunt Mary passed away at ninety-eight years old, we all sighed in relief and exclaimed how wonderful it was that she was finally in a place with her loved ones. Does much of our grief depend on age? Or perhaps it's about how many people we've already lost to the other side?

My Great Aunt Mary was a character. My mother considered her a bonus mom, as she lived in an apartment on the ground floor of my mother's childhood home. Mary never married; instead, she devoted herself to her students, teaching literature and writing for over fifty years. When I was a little girl, she would send me poems, sometimes written on birch bark from our family cabin. I have vivid memories of sharing afternoon tea and pastries with her in her cozy apartment.

Mary was spritely as a young woman. In the 1920s, she bravely traveled to Europe alone. From time to time, she would tell my sister and me stories of her adventures—how she traced a crack on the Liberty Bell or how, as an outsider, she was chased down the steps of a Hitler rally in Nuremberg, Germany, in 1929. Mary lived through some of the greatest challenges of the century: the Great Depression, World War II, Hitler, the Korean War, and Vietnam. Yet, she maintained an optimistic outlook on life and a robust sense of humor.

Years later, while writing, it dawned on me that my Great Aunt Mary and Carolyn shared something in common. They both taught us that joy isn't something you find; it's something you create. It's the moments of absurdity that make life feel less heavy, even in tough times.

Now, we can laugh through our tears, keeping their spirits alive in our memories. We can even laugh without tears, recalling Mary and Carolyn as remarkable, funny, dynamic women. When I think of them, it's their laughter I hear first, a bright, ringing sound that reminds me to find beauty in the ridiculous, grace in the imperfect, and love that lingers long after words are gone.

Words Left Behind — Good Old Aunt Mary

Dear Great Aunt Mary,

I thought of you today when I ran out of Stevia for my morning latte. I used sugar instead and could almost hear your exuberant voice, "It's less harm than expected! Sugar is only 16 calories a teaspoon!" You often said this when we shared afternoon tea in your apartment. Though you've been gone for some time, I think of you as vividly as if it were yesterday.

I felt at peace when you passed. I was living in California when Mom called to tell me you had died peacefully in your sleep. I've always wondered why the death of one person can hit so much harder than another, even when we all know, deep down, that we're moving toward the same end. Perhaps it's the age, the number of losses we've already weathered, or maybe it's something more personal, something deeper. With your passing at ninety-eight, the world seemed a little quieter, like someone had turned down the volume on the laughter and stories that once filled your room.

But even in the quiet, I know you're still with us. You are certainly still with my mom. She often reminds me that you were like a second mother to her during her childhood, especially when she was overlooked because of her sister's disabilities. She recently confessed that you sent her money while she was away at college—a lifeline in countless instances.

Carolyn and I felt a bittersweet relief when we heard you had passed on. We knew you had moved to a place where you could be reunited with the loved ones you had lost, where you could sit with them again, perhaps with your famous four o'clock tea and a story to share.

You were a character, Aunt Mary. Your sweet tooth was legendary, your optimism heroic. You always held a special place in our hearts. I think about how you lived with such grace and independence. You transformed our frigid ancestral Northern Minnesota house into a cozy sanctuary filled with warmth and wisdom. To my mother, you were a constant presence—reassuring, wise, and funny. And to me, you were also something extraordinary—a poet, a teacher, and a woman whose heart was as expansive as the world itself.

I'll never forget the poems you sent me as a little girl, sometimes written on birch bark from the trees at our family cabin. You had a way of making everything feel both grand and intimate, as if the world's biggest stories could be shared through the smallest, most thoughtful gestures.

Your stories, Great Aunt Mary—how could I ever forget them? You told us about your brave solo travels across America and Europe in the 1920s, tracing the crack on the Liberty Bell and, most vividly, being chased down the steps of a Hitler rally in Nuremberg in 1929. You lived through the greatest struggles of the last century, the Great Depression, World War II, and more. Yet, through it all, you kept your optimism, humor, and light. Even in the darkest moments of history, you taught us that joy isn't handed to us, it's something we create from within.

As I've grown older, I've come to understand how true that is. In a world that can feel heavy and overwhelming, you showed us that joy doesn't have to be found; it can be shaped, even in the toughest of times. You taught us to see beauty in the absurd and grace in the imperfect.

Now, as I continue on without you here, I carry those lessons with me. You made the world feel a little lighter and a little more beautiful. You brewed magic tea. Even when I'm sad, the thought of you makes me smile. You taught me that life is remarkable because of its absurdities, that imperfections hold meaning, and that love never truly leaves—it lingers, long after the words are gone.

Aunt Mary, you linger still. In the joy we create, in the beauty we find in the world around us, even in the most unexpected places, like tree bark.

Thank you for being my great aunt—for your stories, your laughter, and your love. I will never forget the legacy of joy you left behind. With so much love,

⌒ Lila

Chapter Six — SURVIVOR

Broadening the Definition of Survivor

"Most of the important things in the world have been accomplished by people who have kept on trying when there seemed to be no hope at all."
— Dale Carnegie

2017

Living through a loved one's terminal illness and eventual death has reshaped me in ways I never could have imagined. I now understand the expression that something could "crack a heart wide open." My relationship with death and grief has made me more empathetic. I am able to connect deeply with the pain of others. This is new to my life, learning to handle emotionally charged situations most people avoid because they feel too heavy or complicated. My sister's death taught me that sometimes, just being present for someone is the most important thing you can offer.

Not long after Carolyn passed, my friend Allison reached out with a request. "Lila," she began cautiously, "I have this friend, Maria. Her husband was just diagnosed with glioblastoma—the same cancer that took Carolyn. She's really struggling. I don't know what to say to her. Would you talk to her?"

"Yes, of course," I said without hesitation. "Have her call me anytime."

Maria called two days later. I remember pulling my gray Ford pickup to the side of the road to take her call. I didn't know much about her, other than that she worked with my friend Allison as a writer for a television show. From the start, Maria came across as a sharp woman who was well educated and deeply informed. She had already researched everything about her husband, Mark's diagnosis, identified clinical trials for which he might be qualified, and narrowed down treatment options to the two best hospitals in the country. Her voice was steady, but beneath it, I could hear her exhaustion and fear.

She told me about their life together—a beautiful twenty-year marriage filled with love and mutual support. Mark had been her rock during years of infertility treatments, and now, even as his world was collapsing, he was still stepping up to care for their young daughter while Maria chased her dream writing job. They'd been thinking about taking a vacation to Hawaii, she said. Then, seemingly overnight, their world cracked wide open.

"It's overwhelming," I said gently. "I remember feeling the same way when Carolyn was diagnosed. It came out of nowhere."

"Yes," she replied, her voice trembling. "It feels like I'm stuck in a nightmare I can't wake up from. Every morning, I hope it's all just a bad dream, but it never is."

"I know," I said softly. "I used to wish for that, too. I spent a lot of long hours staring at my bedroom ceiling fan, wanting to stay in my bed."

Her voice broke as she began to cry. "I just want to make it better. I want him to get better. What am I missing? What more can I do?"

"Oh, Maria," I said, taking a deep breath. "You are the survivor of this story—not Mark. Have you accepted that yet? Has anyone said the truth of what will happen to you and your family out loud? The truth is that you are losing Mark. He is terminal. No one has lived from this diagnosis. He is going to die."

There was silence on the other end of the line, then a sharp intake of breath. Maria began sobbing, and I just sat there, hearing her cry. After a long pause, I continued gently. "It's a horrible truth to hear out loud, but you CAN survive this. You CAN gather all the strength you need to make it through for your daughter. You can teach her how to survive, too. It's hard, but it's possible."

That's a lesson I learned through Carolyn's journey. Losing her shattered me, but it also taught me to live with deeper intention. Pain can become fuel if you let it. I told Maria about how I'd learned to let grief move through me, instead of holding on to it. I shared how, after Carolyn's diagnosis, it took me a long time to realize that survival doesn't just mean enduring. It means finding ways to live fully in the face of loss.

For months after that conversation, I texted Maria regularly. One day, seemingly out of the blue, I sent her this message: "The time is now. Go to Hawaii. Don't wait for the perfect moment, because it'll never come."

She did go, and when she came back, we talked about how much that trip meant to her family. We also talked about the discomfort of receiving help. "It's so hard to accept anything from people," she admitted. "It feels embarrassing."

"I know," I said, laughing. "But think of it like when you had your daughter. Didn't people bring you meals and gifts for the baby?"

"Yes," she said, smiling at the memory.

"And didn't that food restore you? Didn't those gifts save you time?" I asked. "Accepting help now is the same. Let people support you—it's not a weakness. It's a strength."

One of the hardest parts of losing Carolyn wasn't just her physical loss. It was losing all the people who couldn't bear to be around me afterward. People I thought would be there for me drifted away. Some friends couldn't handle the pain of seeing me, knowing I was a living reminder of what we'd lost, Carolyn. I looked like her. I sounded like her. One old friend, of both ours, hung up on me mid-conversation. "I'm sorry," she said through tears. "You sound too much like Carolyn. I can't do this." She never called back. I miss her. I needed her. I wish she had trusted that we could have healed together.

But, I've also found new connections. Starting a nonprofit art foundation in Carolyn's name introduced me to people who loved art and didn't shy away from my grief. I once believed Carolyn's closest friends would stay in our lives, especially for her son. But grief changes people, and not everyone can handle the depths of emotion we traveled to in our grief journey.

Despite everything, the losses, the hurdles, we've found resilience. We now live with greater awareness of what it is we have, the blessings in our lives. We have learned that time is precious, and every moment matters. It's not about waiting for life to get easier—it's about showing up for it, even when it's hard.

Volume 6 — *TENACITY*

"**Mental discipline and tenacity in the face of obstacles are traits that have greatly helped me in both my personal and professional journey.**"
— **Priyamvada Natarajan**

2018

In the depths of my grief, my journal became a lifeline, helping me stay afloat through the despairing waves of sorrow and loss. Encouraged by George, I took a leap of faith and started transforming my fragmented journal entries into the structure of a book. It felt like an insurmountable challenge, unjumbling the raw emotions I'd kept buried for so long as words on the pages of my journal. I would sit down to organize my writing, but would get caught up in reading and the memories and forget the objective I had in my head. I wasn't sure I could create a cohesive body of work on my own. Alex, a friend who had already published a book, introduced me via email to Jenny, an experienced editor. Jenny was like a lighthouse ready to guide me through a storm, her unbiased insights shining a light on the strengths and weaknesses of my writing.

Jenny's critiques were invaluable. They gave me the courage to tackle the daunting task of reworking my very first manuscript. The process wasn't just about writing. It was about baring my soul. "Don't make a messy story clean," Jenny said repeatedly. I had to unlearn what I'd been taught earlier in life—not everything needed to be neat and polished. There was grit and there were uncomfortable truths in my stories. I had to make peace with my erratic process: weeks of silence followed by intense, caffeine-fueled weekends where I poured my heart out onto the page. Writing the most emotional chapters felt like climbing a mountain. I needed time to build courage before I could face them. Jenny's advice was always the same: "Focus on your truth. Don't worry about the audience."

That mantra repeated time and time again in my head. I wrestled with the fear of what my revelations might expose—not just to readers but to myself. But as I delved deeper, I realized something powerful. By sharing the highest and lowest moments of my journey through grief, I was offering others a window into a universal experience. Grief, while deeply personal, connects us all. We all, at some point in our lives, lose someone we love. And sharing our stories, I believe, is one of the most profound ways we can understand one another. It transcends barriers of race, religion, and identity. Stories encapsulate the commonality of humanity.

In the fall of 2019, after months of editing, I took a deep breath and submitted my manuscript to a publishing house that champions female writers. To my surprise—and utter delight—they accepted it. What followed felt surreal: cover designs, a book trailer, and even a website. My journal, my raw outpouring of emotions, had turned into something tangible, something that I could physically hold in my hand.

But just as things were falling into place, my world took another devastating turn. While away on a trip, I got a call about my dear friend Lisa. She'd been feeling off—tired, in pain, chalking it up to what she thought might be a kidney stone. A trip to the ER revealed something far worse. Her boyfriend, Tom, updated me with news that hit me like a ton of bricks: Lisa had cancer.

It was like déjà vu. Carolyn, my sister, had passed not long ago, and now I was staring down the barrel of another major loss. Lisa wasn't just a friend. She was family. We worked together, traveled together, spent holidays together. She had been by my side during my sister's illness, caring for Carolyn like she was her own sister. The thought of losing her was unbearable. As Lisa's health rapidly declined, denial became my refuge. I avoided the hospital, its halls too heavy with memories of past losses. Tom and I clung to humor, spinning wild fantasies to keep the pain at bay. But reality hit hard when the doctors confirmed the cancer had spread everywhere. There was no lung lining left. She was fading fast. I prayed, hard. I pleaded with Carolyn, Grandma Glasoe, my dad—anyone on the other side who might be listening.

"Please," I'd say aloud while driving, "I can't lose Lisa too."

One night, I dreamed of a man—her father, I think—holding Lisa as a baby, blowing air into her lungs to help her breathe. I begged him to intervene, to give us more time. But three weeks after her diagnosis, Lisa was gone.

Her passing plunged me into a familiar void. I lost my appetite, my will to do much of anything. I felt cursed. I thought constantly about her daughter. Her daughter was just one year older than Matson had been when he lost his mom. How could another child lose their mother? It wasn't fair. The fear of more loss consumed me. I obsessed over insurance policies, wills, anything that might protect my family from the chaos of the inevitable. Lisa and Carolyn both lived healthy, bright lives. I worried I was next.

"Please, dear God, don't allow any more loss into the life of my family. Please let me live until the children are grown."

Mundane activities felt fraught with danger. I followed my daughter riding her bike to school in my car, terrified something might happen to her. Eventually, I turned to journaling again. Writing helped me recognize the source of my fear—the anticipation of more loss. With my husband's support, I began navigating the complexities of grief once again. He reminded me that the best way to honor those we'd lost was by continuing to live. It wasn't easy, but the faces of my children—and Lisa's daughter—reminded me that joy could still be found. Amid tears and laughter, I learned to embrace life's unpredictability. The scars of loss, while painful, became a testament to a life fully lived. Each chapter of grief taught me something new about resilience and growth. I now know, without a doubt, that even in the face of unimaginable loss, we can find ways to move forward, to grow, and to connect more deeply with the people around us.

Lisa's funeral was almost unbearable to attend. She had been one of six siblings, and they were all there, gathered to celebrate her life. Each one of them carried a piece of her spirit, and their shared grief was palpable. I knew her sisters well; we had spent memorable moments together over the years. When I arrived, we hugged tightly, holding onto each other as though the embrace itself could ease the ache in our hearts. They knew I had lost a sister too, and in that moment, we stood in the shared, silent understanding of what it meant to lose someone so irreplaceable.

Lisa's daughter was there as well, her quiet strength a testament to her mother's influence. And then there was Tom, Lisa's boyfriend, whose presence had become a steadying force in my own family's life. We had all grown to love him dearly. Seeing him there, trying to stay composed while his heart was clearly breaking, added another layer to the collective grief we all felt.

Yet, amidst the overwhelming sadness, there was a strange comfort in the crowd. The room was filled with people who had loved Lisa—family, friends, colleagues, and neighbors—all united by the profound loss of someone who had touched our lives so deeply. There was healing in being part of such a large group of mourners, in knowing we weren't alone in our devastation.

As memories about Lisa were shared—her humor, her kindness, her unwavering loyalty—it became clear that her absence would be felt by all of us in countless ways. We laughed through tears at the stories shared, celebrated the beauty of her life, and mourned the stark reality that she was no longer with us. It was a bittersweet reminder that while grief can be isolating, it can also bring people together, binding them in love and shared remembrance.

Words Left Behind — My Dear Friend Lisa

Dear Lisa,

It feels strange to write this letter knowing you'll never read it. In the void you've left, I find myself needing to talk to you—needing to hold onto the threads of our connection in whatever way I can. I thought a letter might be the solution. I'm hoping if I write it down, and read it out loud, it may actually reach you.

I've been thinking a lot about the day we met, nearly a decade ago. My sister introduced us, and from that moment, it felt like you'd always been a part of my life. If past lives are real, perhaps we lived a few together. That's how close the connection felt. We had instant friend chemistry. I knew that behind that radiant smile we shared an understanding beyond words. You were another sister. You fit seamlessly into my world.

We had so much in common. Our Midwestern roots defined us—you from Michigan, me from Minnesota. When we talked, I realized we shared an aesthetic and a love for creating beautiful spaces. You weren't like anyone we had ever hired at our design company; you felt like the missing link we had been looking for. Your warmth, patience, and talent transformed our business. I joke that you were my "hired patience," when it came to clients. Everyone who crossed your path adored you.

You had an incredible way of making work feel less overwhelming. I actually looked forward to loading up the truck for pre-design installation with you. I loved shopping with you for inventory. I often look at the picture I hung in our studio of you trying to manage seven shopping carts at a store checkout. I also remember the days when your daughter, Amara, and my daughter, Fliss, would dress up in princess costumes and giggle in the next room while we cooked dinner in my kitchen. Those moments, at work and in our home, were pure magic. Mothering is hard, but with you, it felt a little less lonely.

When my sister, Carolyn, got sick, you were there, giving more of yourself than I ever could have asked for. It felt like we were lifelong friends. Your care for her, and for me, was a lifeline during the dark months of her treatment. How could I ever thank you enough for the meals, the support, the massages that briefly relieved Carolyn's pain, your quiet presence that made unbearable days a little more bearable?

When I started to find my footing again, after Carolyn had passed, you were taken from us. It was a jolt! Your diagnosis was so unexpected. I feel like I still have not fully processed that you are gone. The world feels so much smaller without you. I still catch myself reaching for my phone to call you, to share a funny story or vent about a tough day with design clients. When I remember you are gone, the weight of that truth crashes over me all over again. I haven't seen Amara now in a long while. I am scared I won't see her again for a long time. I think about her constantly. She felt like my girl too. I know she has your strength and your quiet resilience. It is not fair that she has to grow up without you. You were her everything. Lisa, I promise I'll do whatever I can to make sure she knows how incredible you were. I know your sisters and brothers will too.

Your funeral was so tough to attend. It was also a testament to the extraordinary life you lived. Seeing your sister Jackie, Amara, Tom, and everyone else who loved you gathered together was both heartbreaking and healing. You were so loved, Lisa. Know this fact. You still are.

I miss you. I miss your laugh, your kindness, the way you made everything feel a little lighter for me. I've learned so much about grief these past few years—how it never really goes away, but how it shapes and changes everything. You've also taught me about resilience, about the strength it takes to keep going in the face of adversity.

I'm trying to be like you, Lisa—for Fliss, for my family, for Amara, for you.

Thank you for being my dear friend, co-pilot mom, and work partner. Thank you for the love you poured into every moment we shared. You are irreplaceable, and I will carry you in my heart forever.
Always,

 Lila

The dirt was damp, the scent of earth rising as I pressed the trowel into the ground. I could bury grief, or so I told myself. Nothing had prepared me for losing Lisa.

Her laugh used to fill the corners of our office. Now, her absence was a shadow that stretched endlessly across the landscape. Lisa's daughter, Amara, had been whisked away days after the funeral by her father—a man Lisa had never married, a part of her past. He had arrived with a flurry of paperwork and legal jargon, listing her house quickly as the executor of Amara's estate. There had been no space for goodbyes. I wasn't prepared.

My design studio had been our shared sanctuary. Lisa loved to make things beautiful, like I did. She loved organizing—folding the pillow covers and organizing them by color. Amara and Fliss would often help, throwing pillow inserts into the cargo nets we used as pillow storage bins. I hadn't been able to go back to my design studio for many days following the funeral.

I don't know why I'd chosen this particular day, but I woke up with the idea that I had to learn to move forward. Bravely, I dressed, found my work keys, filled my pockets, drank two cups of black coffee, and walked to the front door of our work studio. Newly delivered boxes from vendors greeted me at the entry, shielding me from the emptiness of Lisa. As I picked them up, my hands trembling, I knew what I had to do.

From my pocket, I pulled out Amara's toy, a hand stitched mouse filled with beans by her mother. It had been forgotten in our work truck, before Lisa became ill. It was the only thing Amara had left behind, a forgotten relic in the chaos of a departure, at the end of a long work day when Lisa wasn't feeling well. We'd closed out today's work day earlier than usual. I traced the stitching of the mouse's ears with my finger, remembering Amara's giggles that day, as Lisa pretended the mouse she had made was alive.

I exited the studio door, mouse in hand and dug a hole near the base of the old apricot tree, its roots sprawling like veins through the soil. I could feel the weight of the mouse as I placed it into the ground. The beans made it heavier than expected.

"I don't know if I'll see you again," I whispered, my voice cracking. "But you're here. You'll always be here."

I covered the mouse with soil, pressing it down gently, tucking it in its new grave. And as I did, something loosened inside me—a knot I hadn't known I was carrying.

The grief wasn't gone; I knew it never would be. I realize now that I was physically attempting to bury my grief. I cried and cried. A deep belly cry turned out to be healing in that moment. Suddenly, overlooking the meadow Lisa had loved just outside our design studio, the bean-filled mouse felt less like a weight and more like a seed. Maybe it would grow into something beautiful one day.

Chapter Seven — FINDING MEANING

Reflecting Back on the Greatest Challenges and Celebrating New Achievements from the Journey

"What lies behind you and what lies in front of you pales in comparison to what lies inside of you."— Ralph Waldo Emerson

There's an unexpected magic in revisiting the moments of our past. Sometimes, it brings clarity, other times, humor, but it always feels meaningful to reflect on what has shaped us. For me, so much of my healing has come from remembering and writing down the stories I shared with my sister, Carolyn. We had a childhood filled with imagination and companionship, and I often think about how lucky I was to have her by my side during those formative years.

Our Midwest basement was the setting for countless adventures, especially on snowy days when the outside world felt too cold to brave. With just the two of us and our imaginations, we turned that space into an entire universe. One day it was a bustling school, the next a glamorous salon. Sometimes it even became a roller rink. We'd spend hours in those imagined worlds, laughing and playing, completely oblivious to the passage of time.

Our Norwegian Elkhound, Kari, was an ever-present part of our adventures. She wasn't just a dog; she was a willing participant, often dressed in costumes and, on occasion, taking starring roles in our escapades. One of my favorite memories is the time we transformed our basement into a hospital. Kari became part of the medical staff, dutifully making rounds with us. We laid out pillows along the wood-paneled walls to serve as patient beds, and our "hospital" was soon filled with our dolls and stuffed animals.

Jill, the oversized sock doll, was our most dramatic patient. She had recurring eye problems—her vision mysteriously disappearing throughout the day. Carolyn, the lead surgeon, would diagnose her while wearing a necklace as a stethoscope, and Kari would sniff Jill thoroughly, as if confirming the diagnosis. It was decided: Jill needed eyelash surgery. We threw white aprons over our heads, preparing for the complex operation. Kari was outfitted in one of Dad's oversized undershirts and a pair of Mom's underwear we'd swiped from the laundry room. Carolyn carefully plucked a few of Jill's eyelashes with tweezers, declaring the surgery a success. Post-op recovery turned the hospital into a spa, where Jill could recuperate in style, with Kari serving as the attentive ICU doctor by her bedside.

Reflecting on memories such as these reminded me of the bond we shared. The photo I selected for the back cover of my first book captures us perfectly. In the image, Carolyn and I are dressed in identical camel-hair coats over matching floor-length dresses. We stand shoulder to shoulder, smiling at the camera. It was typical of us—we loved to dress alike and stick together. That closeness only deepened as we grew into adults.

I'll never forget a moment early in Carolyn's motherhood when she turned to me and said, "Promise me, if something happens to me, you'll help Chris with Matson." Her words were sudden and serious.

"Of course," I replied instantly. "I'd expect you to do the same for Fliss."

That's the thing about sisterhood—it's a bond that often grows stronger as life becomes larger. From childhood to partnering and then to motherhood, our lives became intricately connected. Carolyn relocated to be closer to me. We shared the highs and lows of every day, and I knew with certainty that if the time came, I'd step in for her, just as she would for me.

Months after Carolyn passed, I pulled into my driveway late one night and noticed lights on across the street. Through the window, I could see Matson skipping through the living room, an orange throw blanket swirling above his head.

"It's a school night!" I exclaimed as I walked through the door.

"Indeed," my husband Dines whispered, motioning for me to keep my voice down. "Fliss went to bed an hour ago."

"I'm talking about Matson," I whispered back. "He's still up galloping around. I told you Chris and Matson should've stayed here permanently after Carolyn died."

"Babe, they need to figure this out on their own. Give Chris some space," Dines said gently.

I nodded, knowing he was right, but Carolyn's words weighed on me: Promise me you'll help.

A few days later, Mary, Matson's third grade teacher, emails both Chris and I about a meeting she'd like to schedule regarding Matson. It's not regular conference time, so I worry. My earlier fears about Matson's unchaperoned late nights have resulted in serious consequences. Matson's teachers have included me in emails for the past two years, since Carolyn's initial diagnosis. Treatments often took place in Los Angeles and Dines and I filled in as parents for Matson while they were away. Even before Carolyn's diagnosis, travel schedules were erratic due to Carolyn's art dealing career, and Matson became our bonus son quite often. When he was very young, he slept in a Pac-n-Play in my walk-in closet, calling it his "Bedwoom."

Matson's early integration into our home has ultimately become a blessing. Our family feels like it naturally includes Chris and Matson. Fliss refers to Matson, not as her cousin, but as her brother. Matson's school is picturesque. The wood buildings sit on one hundred and fifty acres filled with Oak Trees and meadows. Rock-lined pathways lead from the parking lot to the classrooms. Rocking chairs line the deck space and birds chirp in trees. Mary's classroom is ideal for a third grader. There are bright-colored fabric book holders on the backs of the desk chairs. Student projects and artwork are hung neatly around the room. In one large corner, there are a mass of floor pillows and throw pillows to sit on. This is where Chris and I sit alongside Mary. Her purple shirt matches the purple hue of her dark, long hair. She has multiple folders on her lap, and I can see Matson's name written in all caps down the side of each one.

"How's Matson doing?" she asks with genuine concern. "Sometimes, it's hard enough for kids to just make it to school each day after losing a parent."

"Matson's a great kid," Chris says. "He loves school."

"That's great, Chris," Mary smiles. "Everyone really loves Matson. He seems to be the bridge between the boys and the girls. The girls confide in him, and the boys always seem to include him in all of their activities."

"Great," Chris responds, with a slight laugh.

"I'm calling you in today because Matson seems to be having trouble completing his work. All three areas we are studying have missing homework assignments. I'm wondering if there's a system we could set up to help him manage his time better at home." I immediately flash back to the late night antics I have been witnessing through the windows of Chris's house.

"I think that's a terrific idea," Chris says. "I'm wondering if doing homework with his aunt and uncle may work better." Mary and Chris look at me.

"Yes, totally an option," I say. "I also think trying to get work done before dinner would be a good plan, so Matson could maybe get to sleep sooner." I can see from the look on Chris's face he knows, and I know that Matson has been staying up late at night.

"Sounds like we have a good plan," Mary enthusiastically adds, standing up. Chris and I get up from our floor pillows. Mary walks us to the classroom door, pointing out Matson's artwork over the coat rack as we exit.

"I think Matson may do better staying with you," Chris says as we walk alone down the path and towards the parking lot.

"We'd be happy to do that, Chris," I answer. "Let's figure out details tonight at dinner."

It's funny how timing often works out perfectly. Our new home search, that we were sure would only take three months, has taken almost eleven months. Ever since our move from Los Angeles, in 2006, I have dreamed of living in a Spanish-style home in Ojai. Growing up in Minnesota, a home with a tile roof felt so decadent. The Spanish-style haven we have finally found is warm in character. The exterior boasts that distinctive Spanish stucco charm, painted in a perfect white that reflects the Californian sun. An iconic, red-tiled roof is my favorite aspect of the house and adds a touch of Mediterranean allure. It feels like we are living at the Ojai Valley Inn, a beautiful resort in our small valley that, before we moved to Ojai, we visited each year. This was when we lived in Los Angeles and before we had children. Entering the home, the open layout is welcoming, with an airiness that's quintessentially Californian. The front entry room boasts eighteen-foot ceilings. The living room invites relaxation centered around a natural rock fireplace that extends from floor to ceiling. This will be perfect for cooler evenings. In the kitchen, farmhouse charm takes center stage. White wooden cabinets, walnut floating shelves and wrought-iron accents create an inviting space where I look forward to cooking meals for our family. A patio sits prominently in the center of the house, between the primary bedroom and the kitchen. It promises idyllic moments spent hosting barbecues or enjoying a sunset with a glass of wine. This house is what I have been dreaming of in a new home, laid-back living in beautiful surroundings. It's not just a house; it's going to be a healing sanctuary for our family.

Matson will fit easily into our living plan. We will set up his bedroom from day one. I have had nightstands from his great-grandmother in our storage since I helped clean out her home. I will now use them in his room. Art that was gifted to his mother by a well-known artist will hang over his bed. Its blue color influences me to buy brand new blue bedding, and a multi-colored rug. His large brown teddy bear will be placed in the center of the bed and magically the room will feel like it's perfect for him. Matson's bedroom is located next door to Flissy's room. They will share a bathroom just off the hall. I plan to hang family pictures in the hallway—as many baby pictures of Matson as there are of Fliss. Whitney, our family photographer, is already scheduled to take more pictures of the kids over winter break. It is details like this that will make Matson feel like this is as much his home as ours.

Chris and I make a plan that he will pick up and drive Matson to school most mornings and join us for our evening meal. We started this tradition when Carolyn was alive and we all lived under one roof—summing up our day by listing our "greatest challenge of the day," and "our greatest accomplishment." Traditions are a welcome addition to life in the new house as we begin our new chapter.

Our new family rhythm emerges naturally. Chris joins us for nightly dinners, where we share our "biggest challenge" and "greatest accomplishment" of the day. It feels so good to be together. We began to find meaning in our new configuration, reflecting on the challenges we face and celebrating the small victories that come with them. It isn't easy, but it feels right—like a new chapter written with love and intention.

Volume 7 — *LIFE AMPLIFIED*

"Becoming a mother makes you the mother of all children. From now on each wounded, abandoned, frightened child is yours. You live in the suffering mothers of every race and creed and weep with them. You long to comfort all who are desolate." —Charlotte Gray

2020

I open my email per usual while I have my morning latte. My first book has just been published. I am almost breathless. Friends have already begun pre-buying the book, planning to read my story. There is a note from an old friend of my sister's, Laurie, in my inbox. She has received and read one of the first copies I got from my publisher.

"I just want to say that I think you all did an amazing job in a very tough situation. It must have

been a comfort to your sister, Carolyn, to know that after she was gone, you, Dines, and Fliss would be there to look after Chris and Matson. My mother died when I was eight years old. She had a heart attack in the middle of the night while I was sleeping in bed with her. My 10 year old sister and I were the only ones living with her at the time. Our parents had divorced the year before. I had to call the ambulance and wait for them to arrive. After that we went to live with our father, who was an alcoholic. Our situation was not a good one. We basically raised ourselves and took care of our father also. I have thought about Matson so much in the last few years. He is so lucky to have all of you to also give him all the love he needs to thrive. You will keep the memory of Carolyn alive and through conversations with all of you he will remember and know her. After my mother passed, no one in our family talked about her. It certainly did not help the healing process. That will never be the case in your tribe."

I read and re-read this email again and again. I love that my story is encouraging others to share their stories. It touches my heart. There is another note in my email from a friend of mine.

"I only met your sister once, but now I feel like I have known her all my life and I feel I know you better, too. I lost my older sister to cancer when she was relatively young, as well. But I was living in London and she kept it a secret from our whole family (all except her husband). So although you had to walk the path with Carolyn, I hope you see it as a blessing. I just got a phone call from my brother-in-law asking for my prayers and my sister passed the next day. I respect her decision, but it will always make me sad."

I never expected that my life would look like it does today. My future aspirations always included my sister. When she died, I feared I would never move forward on my own. I also never dreamed I would write a book. It took an extraordinary set of circumstances to propel me to do so. But, the aftereffects of sharing my story, and hearing others' stories in return, are reminders that we are not alone in our human experiences. Our stories can provide motivation, compassion, hope, and comfort to the world. I am so grateful to have discovered the writer inside of me. If my sister had not died, I would not have started an art foundation. The shows we have launched and the artists' careers we have supported through the foundation continue to astonish me. I am braver than I was before experiencing deep loss. I have experienced a journey spanning the depths of grief to the discovery of my resilient self. The world feels different. It's a cliché but the grass does look greener, the flowers do smell more fragrant. My view of life has forever changed. I have changed. At fifty, I am no longer fulfilling aspirations, I am creating new ones. There are no impossible circumstances. We can overcome our biggest obstacles. We can live life amplified by all we've experienced, the good and the bad.

When I was a little girl, I remember the late summer air in Northern Minnesota already feeling cold. At the beginning of August, it definitely felt like fall. My covers were warm and thick—a Hudson Bay blanket over a down comforter and a cozy flannel sheet grounding them all. When I opened my eyes each morning, I would hear noises coming from the kitchen. The cabin, my mother's family's cabin, was built in 1854 and it creaked when anyone walked across the raised floorboards. My mother was always awake before everyone else. Each morning at the cabin started with the smell of the wood-burning stove, which was also used for cooking. I would hear my mother shut the glass paned interior kitchen doors and know the wood stove had been lit, heating the kitchen. I would soon begin to smell eggs frying, bacon sizzling, and toast browning to perfection. I would run from the comfort of my bed into the warm breakfast room as quickly as possible. This is such a poignant memory for me…how it felt to wake up, at six years old, within the walls of my ancestral cabin.

The juxtaposition of this experience with what it feels like to open my eyes now, at fifty-one, is jarring. Now I am the mother. I am the last to sleep and the first to wake. The food fragrances wafting in the morning air are made by me. Sometimes, on an overly gray morning, I make something delicious to seduce the inhabitants of my home out of bed. My nephew, Matson, has to go to school. My husband, Dines, has to work. It is my responsibility to get them up and set the tone for the day. Matson doesn't know it, but I make a point every school day morning to steal a hug. This has to be calculated with a fifteen year old boy. But in the mornings, he is groggy enough to lean his full body into mine and really receive a dose of morning love. He needs this. His father is not the hugging type, and ever since I have had Matson—since seven—I have made it a point to hug him like his mother once did. I choose to show him that I love him every morning with these hugs. Just recently, he has started reaching for me on some mornings, even before I reach for him. He is almost six feet tall now and overwhelms my five-foot-two body frame. I often can't breathe if he is wearing an enormous, oversized hoodie—the rage now with kids this age. I don't tell him I can't breathe. I just sit still in the embrace of his hug until he lets go. At this moment, I often see his first smile of the day. Smiles are rarer at fifteen than they were when he was seven. His smile fills my soul with morning sunshine, which wakes me up more than my two Nespresso shots. I wonder what he imagines when he first opens his eyes and hears me shuffling around in the kitchen, when he smells the eggs or crepes or sausages I cook for him. I hope he wanders into the kitchen with the same desire I did at six—seeking the comfort and security of familiar smells, the warmth of the oven and an impending hug.

My heart is entering a new era. There are so many moments when those around us may need us to hug them or simply hold their hand. When given the opportunity, I have learned how to truly be there for others dealing with grief. I recently said to a friend who was experiencing the pain of a divorce, "I understand what you're going through. I understand you need support. We're going to walk through this together." Her twenty-three-year marriage had ended. She was immersed in grief.

On the other side, I try to share my heart, letting others lend me a hand. I believe that you can always find "your people." Your people will be the ones who understand you, support you, and remind you that you are not alone.

Chapter Eight — STEPPING BACK

Revisiting the Past to Identify Solutions for the Present

"Being deeply loved by someone gives you strength, while loving someone deeply gives you courage." — Lao Tzu

2024

My nephew Matson turned eighteen on Friday. EIGHTEEN! Eighteen is a BIG DEAL. When I asked him a few days before the big day what he wanted to do to celebrate, he shrugged his shoulders and grunted with what I interpreted as an "I don't know."

So, I offered some suggestions:

"Would you like to have a few buddies over?"

"Nah."

"Watch a movie or put a game on?"

"Uh."

"Go out to a special dinner with your dad, Dines, and me?"

"No. Definitely no."

Eighteen is hard to celebrate in a non-embarrassing way. But I was determined to commemorate the day somehow, someway, even if it was small. I took a step back. There were so many years when my birthday celebrations had delighted him. I didn't ask for permission; I just DID.

So, I told his dad to call his best friend Jonas, who, sadly for Matson's sake, had left for college a few days earlier. Thankfully, Jonas was at UCSB—not too far away. We planned a dinner at home: ribeye steaks in a veal demi-glace, just like his mother once made, baked potatoes to placate my vegetarian palate, and a Caesar salad—Matson's favorite. Jonas would arrive as a surprise during the appetizer course of charcuterie, fresh figs, and a goat cheese and herb dip from the local farmers' market.

I took another step back and decided to order floating candles to adorn the ceiling over the kitchen counter that faces the dining room. The scene was just like the scene in Harry Potter, one of his favorite movies from childhood. Under cozy blankets and dim lighting, he and my daughter, Fliss, still rewatch the Harry Potter movies with enthusiasm every winter holiday.

It took me two hours to attach the floating candles to the ceiling with invisible wires—eighteen of them in total. But once they were hung, they were magnificent, flickering just like the movie that inspired them. Matson's eyes lit up with delight when he arrived home Friday evening.

"WHAT?" he said, pointing to the candles and smiling big enough to make his eyes squint and twinkle, just like his mother's once had. He laughed, and I did too.

"Aren't they cool?" I said. He nodded. "Want to try the wand that turns them off and on?"

He nodded again. Suddenly, he resembled the eight-year-old boy I remembered so fondly. The boy who delighted in the events I planned for him.

The birthday went off without a hitch. Jonas showed up, and he and Matson consumed enough steak for four men. We found our rhythm by revisiting the pleasures of the past. It was his last birthday living officially at home as our child. My heart is full from this remarkable day.

Volume 8 — *INTENTION*

"Great leaders are almost always great simplifiers, who can cut through argument, debate, and doubt to offer a solution everybody can understand."
— General Colin Powell

2023

I make it home just before the hard rain. I unlock the heavy steel and glass front door, the porch light barely illuminating the lock. The house is quiet. Even our dogs are silent, somewhere inside. I do not hear the television or music as I normally do. Stillness sits heavily in the cold evening air. I see a light in my bedroom and walk toward it, turning on a small glass lamp as I pass.

My husband, Dines, is stretched out on the bed, headphones on, arms crossed over his chest, looking at his computer. He types something on the keys as I approach.

"Hi," I say, peeking my head over the monitor. He smiles his handsome smile, then lifts his left hand, pointing to the wall, indicating that my nephew is in his room next door.

"We argued," he whispers, removing his headphones and sitting up.

"What about?" I ask.

"Feeding Baby Bear," he responds. Baby Bear is our petite, gray French bulldog. He has been my nephew Matson's companion since shortly after his mother died.

"He was piling his food bowl high," Dines continues. "He's only supposed to get half a cup at night, right?"

"Matson forgot this?" I ask.

"I don't know what happened. He came home in a state of teen angst. Crabby…you could see it on his face. He was in an argumentative mood, and I fell for it."

This is one of those moments that only mothers seem able to solve—like finding the lost shoe no one else can spot under the sofa.

I have learned in my twenty years of mothering to react softly but with intention.

"Dines, the vet said we should increase his food a bit, but only to about ¾ of a cup. Matson was probably responding to that. Regardless, I'll handle it."

I walk out of the bedroom and head toward the kitchen, where Baby Bear's food is stored. I switch on the wall light in the family room and light the gas fireplace. Opening the pantry cabinet, I scoop up ¾ of a cup of food and head to Matson's room.

"You okay?" I say, poking my head around the corner. Baby Bear snorts from the end of the bed, looking up at me in sync with Matson. "Yeah, I barked at Baby Dines," Matson says, referring to Dines with the nickname of endearment he bestowed on him when he was only two years old.

I bring the cup from behind the threshold of the door into the light. "I'm showing you—and Baby Dines—the recommended amount of food for Bear."

I walk in and show him the inside of the cup.

"Okay," Matson says in a defeated tone.

"We have to remember, sometimes when we're crabby, to carefully handle one another," I say, sitting down next to Matson. "Feelings are more important than things."

Matson nods in agreement. I kiss the peach-fuzz softness of his forehead and leave the room.

I repeat this exact scenario with "Baby Dines." I kiss his weathered forehead. As I leave our bedroom, I hear Matson turn on his music. From the back hall, I see Dines removing his headphones.

I walk to the laundry room and throw a load of dirty towels into the washer from the tile floor. The machine begins to hum, filling with water. Baby Bear runs out of Matson's room, barking at the intruder in the laundry room—me. This wakes our other dog, Henry, who bounds clumsily over his long Goldendoodle legs, half-asleep, toward the laundry room.

"No barking," I say calmly as they meet me in the doorway.

The heavy stillness has lifted. The cold silence has left, replaced by the comforting warmth of a predictably chaotic household. Home, as we know it, is restored.

It has taken me years to recognize that the greatest gift Carolyn gave me was the privilege of raising Matson. I have learned to be a "boy mom," not only the mother of a girl. It is a completely different experience.

When my daughter was small, we would take an early morning walk to the local coffee shop. I would give her an empty cup to play with and to occupy her time. I could sit peacefully for a solid hour, sipping coffee, checking emails or reading the news.

Matson was a different baby. I will never forget our first trip to the local coffee shop. My sister and her husband were leaving at dawn, on a trip visiting an artist in Brooklyn. We set up Matson's pack-and-play in our large bedroom closet in the early morning hours, but he was visibly excited to be at our house and wide awake. It was clear he would not be returning to bed. Fliss was still asleep and, not wanting to wake her, I loaded Matson into his stroller and headed down the street to Coffee Connection. Early morning hours were their specialty. I knew there would be other parents there with babies who had also been awoken at sunrise. I ordered my usual almond milk latte and, thinking Matson could easily be occupied with an empty cup, as Fliss had been at his age, I asked the barista, John, for one. Matson grabbed the cup eagerly out of my hand, stared at it for a few seconds, and then threw it across the room with fervor. He barely missed the head of an elderly man, who was quietly reading the local paper.

"That kid has an arm!" John proclaimed in his thick English accent.

"I'm so sorry!" I apologized, racing to pick it up from across the room. Matson giggled, watching me retrieve his first pitch of the day.

"No worries," John called after me, joining Matson in laughter. "I have a few boys of my own."

Rather than staying in the shop, I placed my latte in the stroller's cup holder. "Headed home!" I said to Matson. So much for a leisurely hour at the coffee shop.

Years later, when Matson entered junior high, I befriended another mom who had just moved to town with three boys. We bonded, in the same coffee shop, over shared stories of the boys we were raising. "I couldn't tell why his hair got dirty so quickly," she said about her oldest. "I told him to quit using conditioner, maybe just use the shampoo."

"I'm supposed to use soap on my hair too?" her son had asked. "I thought that stuff was just for you."

"You haven't been washing your hair with soap?" she responded in awe.

"No, I thought soap was just for your body. I thought that shampoo stuff was just for girls," he admitted. We howled!

"My daughter steals my shampoo!" I said through a chuckle. "Oh my gosh, I wonder if Matson knows to use the shampoo? I'd better check when I get home!"

"Do it!" she exclaimed, using her pointer finger to accentuate her point. "And check that he uses soap on his feet too! Boys' feet are a whole separate issue!"

Matson taught me, at a young age, the difference between an excavator and a telehandler. I have also learned the names of more dinosaurs than I knew existed and college football teams from schools all across our country. I am profoundly grateful for this experience, for Carolyn's priceless gift.

Chapter Nine — PARADIGMS

"Paradigms are powerful because they create the lens through which we see the world." — Stephen Covey

2024

My father was an only child. His mother had a hard time each time she became pregnant, and my dad was the only baby who survived in utero until birth. He was premature, but he survived. My grandmother quit trying for more babies once he was born, putting all her energy into raising him. As he got older, he would ask her for a sister.

"We'll name her Virginia Louise!" he would excitedly tell his parents.

Sadly, he never got his wish. Instead, he became very close to his first cousins, Elizabeth and Margaret. They, too, were only children—one the daughter of his mother's sister and the other the daughter of his father's sister. They couldn't have been more opposite. Elizabeth excelled in school and married her high school sweetheart, whom everyone adored. Margaret hated school and was a defiant child. She moved in with her grandparents because her mother considered her "untrainable." Her grandparents were older, and the neighborhood where they lived had become rough over the years. Margaret learned to protect herself in the absence of her mother and the incidental neglect of her elderly grandparents.

I met Margaret when she was already in her fifties. Everyone in the family called her "Toots," and, when I asked why, I was told simply, "Because it fits her." She was very intriguing to me when I was a young child. She lived alone in an apartment above her antique store.

Necklaces she had purchased on her travels hung on her bedroom walls beside neck cuffs from Africa and strands of beaded tile from Portugal. She perfumed herself with egregious amounts of Shalimar perfume and wore her hair in a large bun atop her head. She spent Christmas Eve with us every year, often arriving in a fur cape with a matching fur muff. She would shock my father by giving us gifts like astrology charts and crystals. Her stories were often eye-opening, and my father would criticize them, saying they "weren't appropriate in front of the children."

Toots also worked at an art museum as the executive director's executive secretary. It was an elegant job. She knew everyone in the cultural scene of the Twin Cities and would often bring a guest to our dinners. Her equally artsy friend Linda was a constant. Linda would add elements to Toots's stories and sneak into the back hall bathroom to smoke cigarettes. Linda and Toots both wore heavy eye makeup, which my sister and I would often try to recreate on our faces after their visits. Toots loved to flirt with men and continued doing so into ripe old age.

At eighty, we moved her from Minnesota to be with us in California. She had aged physically—gray hair, a rounder body, wrinkles at her eyes' edges. She didn't seem self-conscious about her change in appearance and still donned the clothing she had worn as a younger woman. Her breasts, now large and pendulous, were often free of the restrictions of a brassiere.

In California, she loved walking to town in incredibly short shorts. She always ordered a dirty martini when we took her out to eat, no matter the time of day. Spotting a handsome man in a restaurant was her favorite pastime. She would fearlessly approach them, throw her arms around their shoulders, and whisper into their ears.

"You are eating the best thing on the menu, aren't you?" she would coo. The men usually reacted politely, perhaps getting a kick out of Toots and her adoration. She would add a few compliments in these encounters before returning to our table.

After my father died, my mother tried online dating. One day, she mentioned scheduling an upcoming coffee date to Toots.

"I'm meeting him at Java Joe's," she relayed over the phone.

"Don't take him to coffee, darling!" Toots retorted. "Take him to your bed."

Toots passed away during the COVID-19 pandemic, not from COVID, just from old age. I had moved her into a nursing home a few minutes from our home. She told me her ashes should be placed somewhere in New York near the Metropolitan Museum of Art. She had loved her visits there as a younger woman. Currently, her ashes sit on my cookbook shelf, over my desk. I haven't planned our trip to New York yet, but I know it will be adventurous.

Toots's death was different from all the other deaths I had experienced thus far in life. I felt no sadness whatsoever. I celebrated her reunion in another realm with her longtime boyfriend, Bob, and her childhood best friend, Mary Ellen. Both had passed before her, and it was clear how deeply she missed them. Her dog, Babe, a pit bull she had rescued as security for her shop, had died too. In her final days, she told me she could feel Babe in bed with her. She had one leg in this life and one already in the next.

Toots was exhilarated to enter her next chapter, despite mentioning that she was apprehensive about seeing her mother again. I was excited for her. She had lived life to the fullest, took risks, worked hard, played harder, and had fun.

Words Left Behind — Toots

Dear Toots,

I am the age you were when we first met. Your perfume still lingers in my mind, that unmistakable Shalimar cloud that announced your presence long before you entered a room and remained long after you had departed. I often think of you when I hear the boldness of a stranger's laugh or when I spot a handsome man across a restaurant. You had fearless nerve and I commend you for utilizing it throughout your life. It's not so easy to be so brave.

Your stories, oh, your stories! They are like treasured old records that replay in my head. The way you defied every expectation other than your own made life seem like an adventure. I wonder how many men you approached in your lifetime, your whispers near their ears, your voice low and conspiratorial. You definitely left them smiling.

You were a paradox, weren't you? Equal parts glamour and grit, unapologetically yourself in every setting. You taught me that life isn't about fitting neatly into someone else's idea of who you should be. It's about living boldly, wearing the eccentric outfit even if no one else dares to, and drinking the dirty martini no matter the hour.

You currently sit a few feet from where I write every day. It feels comforting to have you near me. I promise I'll get you to New York one day, where you felt so alive. You deserve to rest where your spirit once soared.

I think about you walking into your next chapter with the same confidence you brought to every room you entered on Earth. Your hair is still in its signature bun, your laugh is carrying above the noise, and Babe is trotting faithfully by your side. I picture Bob waiting for you, and Mary Ellen too, both grinning ear to ear. You are all young and energetic and you glow in the comfort of having found one another again.

Thank you, Toots, for teaching me that life is meant to be lived fully—without fear, without apology, and with a little mischief along the way. I hope wherever you are, the martinis are strong, the men are dashing, and the music never stops.
With all my love,

～ Lila

Volume 9 — PATIENCE

In 2024, I was reunited with Lisa's daughter, Amara. She appeared out of the blue. Six years earlier, she had been on my mind daily, but lately my soul had given up hope that she would remain part of our lives. I tracked her through friends, hearing occasionally about a camp she had attended or a quick sighting reported by one of my children's friends.

Once, she reached out to Fliss, asking for pictures of her mother. Fliss enlisted my help, and together we sent her dozens of photos from her past. She had been so young when Lisa died, but I hoped some of the images would spark fond memories.

During the COVID-19 pandemic, when so much of the world was shut down, I would often lay in bed wondering where Amara had ended up. Her father had homes in multiple cities, and Lisa's family wasn't in direct communication. I waited patiently for any word about her.

One day, Lisa's sister Jackie called me out of the blue. We had bumped into each other occasionally at the grocery store and had exchanged pleasantries and articles on social media. "Are you home?" Jackie asked. "I have a surprise for you!"

"Yes, we're here," I confirmed. Honestly, I thought Jackie might be dropping off some produce from the local farmers' market. She was a great resource for healthy eating and often shared tips.

Hearing her pull into the driveway, Dines and I stepped outside. Jackie was walking toward us. Her face was so much like Lisa's—different hair color, but almost the same beautiful features and complexion. "I have a surprise," she said, motioning toward her car.

The back door opened, and Amara emerged—six years older than the last time we had seen her. I burst into tears and ran toward her. "Oh my gosh, oh my... Amara!" I screamed. Dines was laughing with joy as he joined us. We formed a huddle on the front walkway, crying and holding each other tightly.

At that moment, my buried grief came to the surface. I hadn't laid it to rest when I buried her stuffed toy. This moment was cathartic; my disenfranchised grief, the sorrow that had gone unacknowledged for six years, finally found expression.

That day, life began to mend. We were surrounded once again by a love we had thought we lost forever. We learned Amara had been admitted to a boarding school in Ojai. She was happy and thriving. Amara bumped into Matson regularly, at high school sporting events and social occasions.

"She's home!" I squealed to Dines when we settled into bed that night. My heart was finally at peace.

My nephew, Matson, is named after my Grandpa Matson. I loved him dearly as a child. He was a handsome man, always fit and dressed in a neatly ironed shirt. When he was young, he was a champion swimmer. He stayed physically fit well into his eighties and was careful about what he ate and drank. He loved my Grandma Vera beyond measure. After she died, he told me that a part of him had died as well. She was his whole world and had been since they were very young.

We would spend summers with him and Grandma Vera at Little Sand Lake, on twenty-one lakefront acres of land that his father had bought as a young man in northern Minnesota. Grandpa Matson built his own cabin next to the original white cabin constructed by his father. His cabin was yellow, and we referred to it as "The Yellow House." I have wonderful memories of picking fresh raspberries with him in the garden he carefully cultivated each summer. He built us a swing that overlooked the garden, and I would sit on it for hours, watching him pull weeds or plant vegetables. Sometimes we fished on the lake in a rowboat. He knew all the best spots. We would pack sandwiches, pick up fresh bait, and sit for hours among the lily pads, waiting for a bite on our hooks.

Grandpa would regale me with stories of his youth when we were at the cabin. I learned that when he was a child, there were two high diving towers in the lake, built by his father and brothers. There was also a tiny house near the shore where his family connected with their Finnish roots by saunaing. The sauna had been rebuilt many times since its first iteration. When I was young, it had a green exterior and pink curtains that my grandmother had sewn for the dressing area window. Many of the decorations at the cabin were handmade by my mother's family. Grandpa Matson was a meticulous carpenter, and Grandma Vera was an expert seamstress and weaver.

Growing up, my mother said it was her father, Grandpa Matson, whom she would wake if she had a bad dream. He was a gentle man, and during the summers, they would make midnight salads from the garden lettuce and bananas and eat them while they worked through the dream. One of eight siblings, I think Grandpa Matson learned to be a great listener growing up in a large family and having to wait his turn. When I was young, if I was upset during those summer weeks, he would pile me into his old Chevy truck and take me to the nearby mom-and-pop convenience shop for a frozen fudge popsicle. Often, this happened after an argument with my sister about sharing clothing or toys. He would tell me stories about his siblings and how he had learned as a young man that relationships were more important than things.

"When you are my age," he would begin, "and you've lost many people dear to you, you won't think about what they had or what you had, but how they made you feel."

Grandpa Matson was so patient. He was often quiet, waiting to speak until he had a poignant reply or observation. He had taught economics and sociology in a high school for many years, raised my severely handicapped aunt, and nursed his wife through stage-four lung cancer. He never seemed frazzled. Looking back, I wonder how, under these burdensome life circumstances, he never lost his cool. My mother told me that her father's family did not believe in fighting in the home. She never heard her parents argue. She believed this was how all families behaved until she met my father's family. They were loud Norwegians who, in contrast to her quiet family, spoke over one another and often yelled to make a point.

Grandpa Matson helped me buy my first car and my first dog, a Bichon Frise I named Olivia. He was a simple man, but he had an overly generous spirit.

When my parents met my husband, Dines, for the first time, my mother remarked on how much he reminded her of her father. I hadn't noticed it, but she was right. I had chosen someone with the same gentle demeanor as Grandpa Matson. I was wise to do so. Dines's patient and loving ways have carried me through the last decade.

I was in college when Grandpa Matson died. He went into the hospital and never came out. He had never wanted to inconvenience anyone, so the way he left this world made sense. He died quickly and quietly. If good deeds follow us into the afterlife, I am sure Grandpa Matson lives like a king.

A week before my sister died, I dreamt of Grandpa Matson. He told me Carolyn would be in his care as she left this world. He wanted to be the one to accompany her. It comforted me to believe this to be true. I think of her now, still close to him, patiently watching over us all.

Words Left Behind — My Beloved Grandpa Matson

Dear Grandpa Matson,

Even though you've been gone for some time now, I find myself thinking about you often. Writing this letter feels like the best way to express the gratitude I have for you and the love that fills my heart when I think of you and our years together. You taught me so many life lessons, and I carry them with me every day.

From a young age, you showed me the value of patience and kindness. You were never hurried, never harsh, even in the face of life's challenges. Your quiet strength and gentle spirit were a constant reminder that calmness and understanding can accomplish so much more than anger or haste. I try to emulate that grace in my own life, especially now as a mother. It's not easy. You set the bar for what it means to be a truly loving and present figure in a child's life.

You also taught me to appreciate the simple joys: the sweetness of a freshly picked blueberry, the beauty of sunlight hitting the still water over a fishing hole, the joy of sitting in a garden, simply watching the world. You showed me how to live in the moment, to find contentment not in grand gestures but in quiet, consistent acts of love and care. Those summers at Little Sand Lake are treasures in my memory of childhood. I can still see you rowing us out on the lake over the lily pads, teaching us about nature—the forest, the birds, the fish (sunfish and walleyes) in the most effortless way.

Your love for Grandma Vera was the most profound lesson of all. In a world that often moves too fast to cherish what truly matters, you demonstrated what it meant to be completely devoted to another person. Even after she died, your love for her never waned. You taught me that love isn't just a feeling—it's a commitment, a promise you keep every day. That example shaped my marriage and deepened my appreciation for Dines's own gentle ways, which so often remind me of you. In moments of frustration or selfishness, I think back to your words, and they guide me back to what matters most. I remember you telling me how important it was to apologize and never go to bed angry. I'm still trying to manage that!

Thank you, too, for watching over Carolyn. I know, in my heart, that she is in your safe care. When I dreamt of you before she passed, I felt immense comfort knowing you were there to guide her. It helped me deal with the pain of her loss. I picture you both together, perhaps sitting by a lake or taking a long walk. It soothes me to imagine her in your company, feeling the peace and safety that you always brought to me.

Grandpa, your life was a gift to everyone who knew you, and your legacy continues through your great grandchildren. We share with them the lessons you taught. I hope you know how deeply you are missed, how often you are remembered, and how much you are loved. I bet you get a kick out the fact that Matson is named after you. I hope you feel my gratitude for everything you gave to me—not just what you did, but who you were. You've left a lasting mark on my life, and for that, I am forever grateful.

With love,

~ Lila

Chapter Ten — CHOOSING TO LIVE FULLY

My thirties were a life-changing decade for me and most of my friends. We had entered a phase of life where we suddenly found ourselves in a very adult world. There were years when my husband and I attended over ten weddings. Our friends were coupling up, buying homes and dogs, and, more often than not, trying to have babies. The parameters of life had completely shifted. Carefree bar hopping and last-minute trips to Las Vegas were relics of the past. We found ourselves making sensible household budgets and choosing vacation destinations based on what would best entertain our children.

I started hosting Christmas at our house rather than traveling to see my parents. This was an easier plan with kids. Traveling was fraught with the hassle of transporting Pack 'n Play sleepers and car seats on planes and in rental cars. Our daughter slept better in her bed at home, than in a guest bed at someone else's house. Sleep was everything. If she couldn't sleep, that meant we wouldn't sleep, and the trip would be a disaster. My sister had also relocated to California, which meant there were more relatives on the west coast than in Minnesota.

I think of this era of our life as "the good old days." No one in our friendship circle had yet divorced, beautiful babies were being brought into the world, and I hadn't even heard the word "cancer" in relation to anyone my age. There also wasn't yet a wrinkle on my face or a gray hair on my head. We had a lot of fun. Little kids say the cutest things, and as a parent, I saw the world in a whole new light. I remember when Fliss turned four, and we started to talk about preschool. She looked at me one afternoon and said, "Mom, do you remember when I was a whittle (little) kid?"

"I do," I replied, holding back my laugh. "Does that feel like so long ago?"

"Yeah," she casually answered. "That was a really long time ago."

Dines and I had decided to concentrate our parenting efforts on one child rather than having a second one. We loved our little three-person family and our moments devoted just to her. Looking back, I think neither of us were really "baby people." We couldn't wait until Fliss could talk and communicate her needs. The older she got, the more connected we felt as parents.

I had friends who were the opposite. One friend, Jen, loved babies. She had a beautiful little girl, followed by a set of twins and a fourth child shortly after. She confessed to wanting a fifth, but her husband had kiboshed the idea. She was wonderful with babies. Had it been solely up to her, I'm sure she would have had at least six.

My childhood friend Susie decided she wanted two children. Her daughter was one year younger than Fliss. She found out early on that her second child would be a boy. I was so excited for her and her husband Todd. He seemed like the perfect "boy dad." Todd loved being at the beach. He was a dynamic parent to his daughter, beloved by all of her friends.

"These kids are gonna surf!" he proclaimed when Fliss and his daughter were still in swim diapers and trying to eat sand. It was fun to buy Susie a baby gift for a boy. Our world was so girl-oriented, and Fliss loved very feminine things. Dines, a Hot Wheels collector since childhood, was already suggesting which toy cars I could add to our baby gift.

"Hold your horses, honey," I laughed. "He's not even here yet!"

We had a big group of little girls in our friendship circles. I hadn't realized Dines would be so excited about a boy.

Susie's nine months went swimmingly, much like her first pregnancy. She was an adorable pregnant woman—so petite everywhere but her belly. In contrast, I had been really puffy. I had carpal tunnel during my pregnancy and slept with wrist braces. I was so short-waisted, and was bursting with a baby inside of me.

"You are the largest pregnant woman I have ever seen!" my sister exclaimed, like only a sister could, seeing me in my final month of gestation.

Susie lived a few hours from our home, and the day she went into labor, her friend called to let me know she was having her son. All morning, I thought of her. At lunch, Dines and I talked about choosing good dates to meet the baby. My phone rang as I was finishing my last bite of Caesar salad. I saw the call was from San Diego—the same number I had seen earlier in the morning.

"Dines, I gotta take this," I said, springing up from my seat and heading outside the restaurant. "It's someone calling about Susie. The baby's here, I bet!"

That call began one of the most devastating conversations of my life. Susie had had her baby, but he had suffered an embolism while leaving the birth canal and died.

I began sobbing, and soon Dines, who had seen me almost collapse through the window, was holding me as I wept into the phone. All I could think about was my dear, dear Susie, my friend since fourth grade. Sweet Susie, my childhood camp buddy.

"How could this have happened?" I bellowed at Dines through my tears. "Susie didn't deserve this! And oh my God, how will they tell their daughter? How can they get past this?"

Susie and Todd had a private funeral for baby Reid. Every year, on his birthday, she sends out a reminder on social media of the age he would have been had he lived. She and Todd have stayed married. They were brave enough to have another baby, a boy, a few years after losing Reid. At the time, I could not imagine how she would get past their enormous loss. Nothing compares to the grief of losing a child.

This was the beginning of the end of "the good old days." Life caught up with all of us. We cannot escape tragedy in our lives, no matter how hard we try. We don't know what will happen to whom—what marriages will survive, who will get sick, and who will die. We learn that if we want to keep moving forward, we must be resilient in order to navigate life's difficult happenings.

I am so proud of Susie for choosing to live fully and for reminding us all yearly, on Reid's birthday, how lucky we are to be alive.

Words Left Behind — Sweet Susie

Dear Susie,

I've been thinking about you so much lately. Our close friends are having their first grandchild. How is this possible? When did we get this old? They had a scare the last few days. Their daughter had an emergency C-Section after thirty-two hours of labor. I thought about you and Reid and I felt fearful that once again a beautiful baby would be lost and another family would be devastated. I just received a call that the baby, George, and his mother are doing well and I cried with relief. I also felt compelled to write you a letter—to put into words what my heart has carried for years. You have always been a dear friend to me, but what you've shown in your life, your resilience, and your ability to find light even in the darkest times, has deepened my admiration for you in ways I can barely articulate.

I think back to the days we spent as kids, laughing in our cabin, after "lights out" at Cathedral of the Pines Camp and sharing our dreams about the lives we'd one day lead. I never imagined that life would bring such challenges. I lost my sister when she was only forty-six, and I raised her son along with my daughter. You lost Reid in an unimaginable tragedy—something no one should have to endure. I remember the afternoon when I heard the news about Reid, the utter devastation I felt for you, and how helpless I was to make anything better for you.

You have not just endured. You have lived. You have carried the weight of grief with such grace, somehow finding room in your heart for hope and love again. You honored Reid beautifully by sharing your experience with the world, by ensuring that he remains a part of our collective story, and by showing us all the depth of your love.

Your courage to continue, to open your heart after unspeakable loss, is a testament to the incredible strength inside of you. I am in awe of your ability to take each day as it comes, to love your husband, to parent your children with joy, and to show up for those around you. You have sweetly remembered Dines and me on our birthdays every year since we got married. I love receiving your cards, often full of confetti, family pictures, or a silly token. Thank you for thinking of us with such touching generosity.

Susie, you have shown everyone that life can change in an instant, that life is precious. You have demonstrated by how you live that we must celebrate simply being alive. I love you, my friend.
Always,

~Lila

EPILOGUE

Volume 10 — WHAT IF?

"I wanted a perfect ending. Now I've learned, the hard way, that some poems don't rhyme, and some stories don't have a clear beginning, middle and end."
— Gilda Radner

What if anything is possible? Losing so many loved ones has made me contemplate what happens when you die. What if you don't know you have died? Could you find yourself flying quickly through outer space—like I do, in many of my dreams—through a tunnel of blackness? Could we be dead but imagine we are only dreaming?

I wonder, if this happens, what my natural reaction might be. Would I try to wake myself up? Or would I curl into a tight ball in fetal-position and continue on with the journey?

It is easy to imagine believing I'm in a dream, rather than dying. Instead of curling up, I want my arms and legs to extend like a jumping jack or a giant letter X. I've already dreamt of myself, a few times, in this position—floating in space.

What if we imagine wise words in our head as we are dying—so sagacious that our thoughts can direct our body toward the destination we wish to reach? In my dreams, my eyes close and I manifest my arrival at a desired destination. Is it possible, however, to choose a person to whom I might send my coordinates? Perhaps someone I've lost in this life, someone I feel destined to see again? Clearly, when I die, there are no places I will dream of seeing as much as people. Magically, imagine that when we finally stop floating through the darkness, we will be met by those we have missed for so long.

In my creative brain, the afterlife is like the galaxy—so vast that, in human terms, we can't even begin to comprehend its size. I wonder if my curiosity might try to take it all in. Is that even possible? Perhaps there is just one area where we will be assigned. Will I know God is somewhere in this enormous nebula—or, at the very least, feel a power I can identify as higher than myself? I wonder if I will feel, in this realm, that there is something or someone to report to.

I once had a dream where my sister showed me she was very busy in her afterlife. It made me conclude that if you want to continue to work in your afterlife, you can. There must be enormous think tanks where she is, like those we have in Washington, D.C., but bigger than our largest universities. Even the Vatican must be minuscule compared to the temples in the afterlife.

I want to believe that if I wish to watch over the loved ones I left on Earth, I can do that too. Perhaps there will be enough time to create any plan I desire. As the years pass, I'm sure I won't feel the pull to revisit my earthly life or loved ones as much. After a few generations (which may feel like only two minutes in the afterlife), I know my focus will shift to my new existence—hopefully to my unburdened life in this place, free of the constraints of time. Are there endless opportunities in the afterlife to create whatever is dreamed up?

I think that even though we won't really care what we look like when we die, we will appear as our best self. When I dream about my sister, she is always young, vibrant, and beautiful. When you are unhindered by anything, presenting as your best self is possible.

It's clear to me that the anticipation of death is worse than death itself. We say to friends who have lost loved ones after long bouts of illness, "I'm so glad they are now free from their pain." One would think we'd step forward, more easily, into death when called if we were certain we were definitely headed to a better place. A place where football fields of our people are waiting to see us, the ones who loved us most standing on the front lines.

Are there dogs, I wonder? Animals in the afterlife? In my dreams, there are dogs, cats, birds, and countless other spirits waiting to greet loved ones. This will be a new sphere—far greater than we can even begin to imagine. Here, perhaps, our purpose is revealed, and we will speak and move with intention.

I want us to transform. I know that wherever we become more intentional we will grow stronger. We have the power to do anything. Now is the time. Live at Volume 10. Do it today, before you die. Amplify your life.

Bibliography

1. Maya Angelou, Bill Moyers Journal: A Conversation with Maya Angelou, YouTube video, n.d., https://www.youtube.com/watch?v=zr&Sxv9RSdM.

2. Tara Brach, *True Refuge: Finding Peace and Freedom in Your Own Awakened Heart* (New York: Bantam, 2012).

3. Brené Brown, "The Practice of Story Stewardship," Brené Brown Blog, December 5, 2021, https://brenebrown.com.

4. Dale Carnegie, ed., *Dale Carnegie's Scrapbook: A Treasury of the Wisdom of the Ages* (New York: Dale Carnegie & Associates, 1959).

5. Pema Chödrön, *When Things Fall Apart: Heart Advice for Difficult Times* (Boston: Shambhala Publications, 1997).

6. Stephen Covey, *The 7 Habits of Highly Effective People: Powerful Lessons in Personal Change* (New York: Free Press, 1989).

7. Ralph Waldo Emerson, "Self-Reliance," 1841.

8. Charlotte Gray, "Mother to All," Attachment Parenting International Blog, accessed July 11, 2025, https://attachmentparenting.org.

9. Martin Luther King, Jr., speech, Washington, DC, February 1968.

10. Lao Tzu, Tao Te Ching, public domain translation.

11. Jack Maden, "Dancing with Nietzsche," Philosophy Break, October 2018, https://philosophybreak.com.

12. Arthur Miller, residency at Southern Methodist University, Meadows School of the Arts, workshop and production of All My Sons, 1991.

13. Priyamvada Natarajan, "Yale Astrophysicist Priyamvada Natarajan Wants You to Quit the Mansplaining—It's Just Too Boring," Quartz, January 15, 2018, https://qz.com/work/1176791/yale-astrophysicist-priyamvada-natarajan-wants-you-to-quit-the-mans-plaining-its-just-too-boring.

14. Barack Obama, quoted in public domain presidential speech, [exact date unspecified].

15. Colin Powell, quoted in Oren Harari, A Leadership Primer, GovLeaders.org, accessed July 11, 2025, https://govleaders.org.

16. Fred Rogers, "Interview, Part 7 of 9," Television Academy Interviews, accessed July 11, 2025, https://televisionacademy.com.

17. Eckhart Tolle, *The Power of Now: A Guide to Spiritual Enlightenment* (Novato, CA: New World Library, 1997).

About the Author

Lila Glasoe Francese was born in Minneapolis. She is a graduate of Breck School and attended SMU's Meadows School of the Arts in Dallas, earning her Bachelor of Fine Arts Degree in 1994. Relocating to LA, Lila began writing, sold a screenplay (Peg & Shirl), provided character voices for animated television shows (the most notable Family Guy), renovated real estate, and ran the personal lives of producers, studio heads, and CEOs. Lila is the recipient of a McKnight Fellowship, the Wellesley Book Award and most recently An Independent Press Award — Distinguished Favorite 2021 for her book *The Situation: A Radical Journey Thru Sisterhood*. She appeared professionally in regional theatre in both Minneapolis and Los Angeles. Lila began a design house called OHI HOME in 2006 which she continues to run alongside her husband Dines. Her interiors have been published in *Architectural Digest South America*, *LA Yoga Magazine* and *Ventana Magazine* among others. In 2016 Lila helped found The Carolyn Glasoe Bailey Foundation (CGBF). This nonprofit art charity funds artists and provides art education programs in schools and an artist residency program through the foundation's initiative The Ojai Institute. Lila currently lives with her family in Ojai, CA.